The Gospel of Christmas

The Gospel of Christmas

by

J. HAROLD GWYNNE

WM. B. EERDMANS PUBLISHING CO.

Grand Rapids, Michigan

1938

PRINTED IN THE UNITED STATES OF AMERICA

TO MY WIFE

and

OUR CHILDREN,

RUTH LAIDLEY GWYNNE, age 7 years, 6 months
JOHN HAROLD GWYNNE, JR., age 4 years, 7 months
JAMES CALVIN GWYNNE, age 3 years, 5 months

*Who have helped me to see more clearly
the meaning of Christmas,*

THIS BOOK OF CHRISTMAS

is

AFFECTIONATELY DEDICATED

Contents

PART ONE

PART TWO

PART THREE

PART ONE

THE FIRST CHRISTMAS SONGS

Hark! The Herald Angels Sing

Hark! the herald angels sing,
"Glory to the new-born King;
Peace on earth, and mercy mild,
God and sinners reconciled!"
Joyful, all ye nations, rise,
Join the triumph of the skies;
With the angelic host proclaim,
"Christ is born in Bethlehem!"
  Hark! the herald angels sing,
  "Glory to the new-born King!"

Christ, by highest heaven adored;
Christ, the Everlasting Lord!
Late in time behold Him come,
Offspring of the Virgin's womb:
Veiled in flesh the Godhead see;
Hail the Incarnate Deity,
Pleased as man with men to dwell,
Jesus, our Emmanuel.
  Hark! the herald angels sing,
  "Glory to the new-born King!"

Hail the heaven-born Prince of Peace!
Hail the Sun of Righteousness!
Light and life to all He brings,
Risen with healing in His wings.
Mild He lays His glory by,
Born that man no more may die,
Born to raise the sons of earth,
Born to give them second birth.
  Hark! the herald angels sing,
  "Glory to the new-born King!"

—REV. CHARLES WESLEY, 1739.

I

The First Christmas Songs

PSALM 98:1, *O sing unto the Lord a new song; for he hath done marvellous things: his right hand, and his holy arm, hath gotten him the victory.*

CHRISTMAS and songs go together. The first Christmas brought songs of hope and joy into the world that had never been heard before, and that have never since died out. Songs of the Nativity have been sung in all ages, in all languages, and in all lands. Psalms, hymns, canticles, and carols are vibrant with the music and melody, the joy and hope of the Christmas message.

Do we really know the Christmas Songs that welled forth from the hearts of those to whom the fact and meaning of the Nativity were first revealed? It is the message of these first Christmas Songs that we are now to consider.

These Songs are four in number. They are all found in the Gospel of Luke: three of them in the first chapter and one in the second chapter. Three of them have familiar Latin names and have been sung for many centuries as the chief canticles of the Christian Church. These familiar Songs are the 'Magnificat' or Song of Mary; the 'Benedictus' or Song of Zacharias; the 'Nunc Dimittis' or Song of Simeon. The less familiar one is the Song of Elizabeth. There is also the Song of the Angels which was heard by the shepherds, but it should be considered apart from these Songs that came from human hearts.

Two of these Songs were sung by women and the other two by men. One was the Song of an elderly mother of Israel; one the Song of a young mother; one the Song of an aged priest, and one the Song of a venerable saint. All of the Songs came from godly hearts. The Song of Elizabeth breathes the spirit of homage and adoration; the Song of Mary glows with the purity and humility

13

of her devout spirit; the Song of Zacharias reveals his righteousness and faith, and the Song of Simeon exemplifies the spirit of patience and hope that formed a vital part of the age-long dream of all true Israelites.

I. The Song of Elizabeth.

The occasion of the Song of Elizabeth was a visit paid to her in her own home in the hill-country of Judah by Mary shortly after she had received the promise of the birth of a son. When Elizabeth heard the salutation of Mary she was filled with the Holy Spirit, and uttered a psalm of blessing upon the mother and upon the child. She also expressed wonderment at her own honor in thus being saluted by the mother of her Lord. She pronounced a blessing upon Mary for her faith, and declared the certain fulfilment of the things which had been made known to her. The salutation of Elizabeth "was that of a mother to a mother—the mother of the 'preparer' to the mother of Him for whom he would prepare. To be more precise: the words which, filled with the Holy Ghost, she spake, were the mother's utterance, to the mother, of the homage which her unborn babe offered to his Lord." "Blessed art thou among women, . . . And whence is this to me, that the mother of my Lord should come unto me? . . . And blessed is she that believed; for there shall be a fulfilment of the things which have been spoken to her from the Lord." This is the Song of Elizabeth, a hymn of blessing, honor and faith.

II. The Song of Mary.

When Elizabeth had concluded her salutation, Mary straightway uttered her Song. It is not so much a reply to Elizabeth, as it is an answering hymn of homage to God. It is a lyrical meditation, an inspired utterance of personal emotions and experiences. A psalm of moral and spiritual elevation, it is modelled upon the Old Testament Song of Hannah, and it is a perfect mosaic of familiar phrases taken from the Law, the Psalms, and the Prophets. The Song is composed of four stanzas or strophes. The general theme is that of the mercy and grace of God to Mary as an individual and to her people Israel. In the first stanza she blesses God for His favor upon herself, in that she, the bride of a humble carpenter, should receive the highest honor a human being could receive. All generations would call her blessed. Elizabeth had already called her blessed, and this would be continued throughout all generations. While realizing the great honor bestowed upon her, she is conscious of her unworthiness; and while recognizing what it will cost her, she declares her submission as the true hand-maid of the Lord. Her humility and faith are nothing short of sublime.

In the second stanza, Mary dwells upon the character of God, as revealed in His gracious gift to her and to Israel. She praises God for His power, His holiness, and His mercy revealed to all generations of those who fear Him.

In the third stanza, Mary describes the effects to be produced by the Messiah in the future. These results of His coming are set forth in the form of three distinct contrasts. The *proud* will be scattered; the *humble* will be helped. The *high,* that is tyrannical rulers, will be put down; the *low,* that is the oppressed poor, will be exalted. The *rich* will be sent away; the *poor* will be filled with good things. All of these results will be spiritual as well as material.

In the last stanza, Mary emphasizes God's faithfulness to His ancient promises made to Abraham and to his seed for ever, and now brought to fulfilment in the gift of His Son. Mary's Song is a beautiful hymn that voices the fulfilment of the highest hopes and aspirations cherished by the true people of Israel throughout the centuries.

III. The Song of Zacharias.

The occasion of the hymn of the priest Zacharias was the pre-sentation of his new-born son in the temple on the eighth day for the rite of circumcision, and the divine bestowal upon the child of the name John. This Song of Zacharias, called the "Benedictus,' is the hymn of a priest. The hymn spiritualizes a great part of the most ancient Jewish prayer, the so-called 'Eighteen Benedictions'. A great portion of these prayers was said by the priests as a part of their regular religious duties. Zacharias had apparently medi-tated upon, and learned to understand what he had so often re-peated. The leading thoughts of the 'Eighteen Benedictions' in the prayers of Israel were as follows: "God as the *Shield of Abraham*; He that raises the dead, and *causes salvation to shoot forth;* the *Holy One;* Who graciously *giveth knowledge;* Who taketh pleas-ure in *repentance;* Who multiplieth *forgiveness;* Who *redeemeth*

Israel; Who *healeth their* (spiritual) *diseases;* Who *blesseth the years;* Who *gathereth the outcasts of His people;* Who loveth *righteousness and judgment;* Who is the *abode and stay of the righteous;* Who *buildeth Jerusalem;* Who causeth the *Horn of Salvation to* shoot forth ; Who *heareth prayer;* Who *bringeth back His Shekinah to Zion;* God the *Gracious One,* to Whom praise is due ; Who *blesseth* His people *Israel with peace."*

Many of these thoughts are woven into the 'Benedictus' of the priest Zacharias. His song is composed of five stanzas or strophes. The first blesses God for the redemption of Israel, through the Messiah, the Son of David, Who is a manifestation of saving power. The second dwells upon Israel's salvation from all her enemies, as promised through the prophets and cherished by the fathers as God's covenant with His people. The third emphasizes God's covenant with Abraham, with its promise of deliverance from political oppression, to the end that Israel might be free to serve God as a holy and righteous nation. The fourth is concerned with the mission of John the Baptist, the prophet of God, who as forerunner of the Messiah, would proclaim salvation by the remission of sins. The last stanza leads up to the mission of Christ and the blessings He would bring to His people. The source of these blessings is "the tender mercy of our God." Their essence is a visitation of "the dayspring from on high," when the Sun of righteousness shall shine upon those who "sit in darkness and the shadow of death." "Such is the hymn of Zacharias, a hymn of faith, of hope, of gratitude, a song of the salvation provided by the love of God in Jesus Christ our Lord."

IV. The Song of Simeon.

The occasion of the Song of Solomon was the presentation of Jesus in the temple at the age of six weeks. Simeon was a venerable man of Jerusalem who was righteous and devout and whose spiritual hope was set upon 'the consolation of Israel'. It had been revealed to him by the Holy Spirit that he should not see death before he had seen the Lord's Christ. When Mary and Joseph brought the child Jesus into the temple, the aged Simeon received the little babe in his arms and blessed God, saying:

"Now lettest thou thy servant depart, O Lord,
According to thy word, in peace;
For mine eyes have seen thy salvation,
Which thou hast prepared before the face of all peoples;
A light for revelation to the Gentiles,
And the glory of thy people Israel."

In this "sweetest and most solemn song of the nativity," called the 'Nunc Dimittis', the venerable saint employs the figure of speech of the "faithful watchman who welcomes with joy the hour of his dismissal, for he has caught the vision of the coming One; now he is about to be sent away in the peace of an accomplished task, in the peace of fulfilled hope; for his eyes have seen the Saviour according to the promise of the Lord." This Song is broader in scope than the 'Magnificat' or the 'Benedictus', in that it promises redemption not only to Israel but to all the world. The Lord's Christ, the Messiah, is to be a light to reveal the way of salvation to the Gentiles, as well as the true glory of the favored people, Israel.

But while this salvation was provided for all, it would not be accepted by all. To the wondering mother, Simeon added this tragic word of prophecy: "Behold, this child is set for the falling and the rising of many in Israel; and for a sign which is spoken against; yea and a sword shall pierce through thine own soul; that thoughts out of many hearts may be revealed." That is, the ministry of Jesus will be the occasion for the fall and rise of many. The attitude of the people toward Him will be a revelation of their character. Those who reject Him will condemn themselves. This rejection will reach its climax at the cross, when bitter anguish, like a sword, will pierce the soul of Mary. By accepting or rejecting Jesus, men will reveal their true character. The thoughts out of many hearts will be revealed.

V. Practical Lessons From the First Christmas Songs.

Let us consider some of the practical lessons that are to be gained from these original Christmas Songs. First, we observe that Christmas is intended to bring songs to the human heart. It did bring songs to those who first understood its meaning, and it continues to do the same to-day. Elizabeth and Mary and Zacharias sang their songs of faith and joy before the child Jesus was born. At the time of His birth, the angel choir from heaven sang their anthem of praise, glory and peace. The shepherds who heard "the good tidings of great joy" and the song of the angelic hosts returned glorifying and praising God. The Wise-men, when they saw the star that guided them to the object of their quest, "rejoiced with exceeding great joy".

So it has been throughout the more than 1900 years of Christian history, and so it is to-day. All humble people everywhere who know the meaning of Christmas and who have received God's gift of love to the world have unfailing songs of hope and peace and joy in their hearts. Furthermore, these songs abound even in days that are dark and in times that are full of trouble and adversity. The song of the angels was first heard in the darkness of midnight, and their celestial music continues to be heard even in the darkest night by those who have ears to hear.

In the second place, we observe that the songs of Christmas spring only from godly hearts. We have already seen how preeminently true this is of Elizabeth, Mary, Zacharias and Simeon. Their songs were the songs of pure, humble, believing and godly hearts. They were the true Israelites, the true seed of Abraham, the true people of God. They kept alive in their hearts the noblest tradition fostered by Israel throughout the centuries. They were the incarnation of that true piety that had come to perfect flower at the end of the ages of expectation, longing and hope in God. Their souls were fashioned as perfect instruments to give to the world the lofty and undying music of the Christmas message.

Are we as keenly aware of the fact as we ought to be that *unbelief* has no songs of hope or joy to give to the world? Do you recall the strange thing that happened to Zacharias when the angel of the Lord announced to him the promise of a son? Zacharias did not have faith to believe the promise, and for his show of unbelief he was stricken dumb, so that he could no longer speak. Later, when the child was born and when the name John was bestowed upon him, Zacharias' speech returned and he spake, blessing God. His unbelief rendered him mute; his faith gave him the song of blessing and benediction. It is ever so. Unbelief is silent, mute, dumb, as far as songs of praise and blessing are concerned. Faith alone has songs of gratitude and joy and hope. Lord, increase our faith!

What songs do we have from the unbelieving Israelites of Jesus' day? What songs from the wicked Herods who tried to slaughter the infant Jesus, and to exterminate the Christian Church? None at all! They are silent, mute, speechless! They have nothing to give to us in our need; they have no songs to fill our souls with joy and hope and gladness. The unbelieving world has always tried to destroy the Songs of Christmas. Some of the most brilliant minds of the ages have been arrayed in hostile criticism against the sweet and simple and trustful story of Christmas. There are brilliant men in our land to-day who oppose and deny and ridicule the Christian faith. Do they think to destroy the Songs of Christmas by their hostile criticism and their wicked unbelief? Strange, is it not, that the Church has outlived all of the prophets of its doom? The Songs of Christmas will never die because they come from God, and because they find a universal response in the human heart.

If we would have the Songs of Christmas in our hearts and lives, we must have faith in God and faith in Him for Whom Christmas is named. We must love Him and trust Him and wait upon Him. All of our expectation and desire must be centered in Him. We must live pure and godly lives. We must serve the Lord with joy and singleness of heart. If we do this, we will know the meaning in our hearts of the sweetest songs that ever ascended from earth to heaven, and that ever came from heaven to earth.

THE CHRISTMAS OFFER

Joy To The World!

Joy to the world! the Lord is come:
    Let earth receive her King;
Let every heart prepare Him room,
    And heaven and nature sing,
    And heaven and nature sing,
And heaven, and heaven and nature sing.

Joy to the earth! the Saviour reigns:
    Let men their songs employ;
While fields and floods, rocks, hills and plains
    Repeat the sounding joy,
    Repeat the sounding joy,
Repeat, repeat the sounding joy.

No more let sins and sorrows grow,
    Nor thorns infest the ground;
He comes to make His blessings flow
    Far as the curse is found,
    Far as the curse is found,
Far as, far as the curse is found.

He rules the world with truth and grace,
    And makes the nations prove
The glories of His righteousness,
    And wonders of His love,
    And wonders of His love,
And wonders, and wonders of His love.

—REV. ISAAC WATTS, 1719

11/30/47

II

The Christmas Offer

JOHN 1:11-12, *He came unto his own, and they that were his own received him not. But as many as received him, to them gave he the right to become children of God, even to them that believe on his name.*

A S THE holiday season approaches, the world of advertising becomes flamboyant with innumerable attractive Christmas offers. The current magazines are brightly sprinkled with 'Wonderful Christmas Offers' and with 'Marvelous Gift Opportunities'. The commercial world calls into play every possible scheme of advertising technique and every ounce of high-pressure salesmanship ability to entice the public to buy its 'unexampled' and 'unparalleled' Christmas offers. These things may be all right in their place, but the trouble is the commercialization of Christmas is proving to be like the fable of the Camel's Nose— whose bulky owner, you will recall, crowded the master out of the tent! So the American spirit of over-doing the materialistic side of Christmas threatens to crowd the real Christmas out of the tent! It is timely, therefore, to turn our thoughts to the *real* Christmas and to the *real offer* Christmas makes to each one of us and to the world.

I. The Christmas Offer.

Here is John's marvelous description of the Christmas offer: "He came unto his own, and they that were his own received him not. But as many as received him, to them gave he the right to become children of God, even to them that believe on his name." What is the real Christmas offer? It is the gift of God's love to the world, even His only begotten Son, Jesus Christ. He is the eternal Word of God. He is the light and life of men. He is the One through whom the world was made. He is the revealer of the Fath-

23

er's glory; the bringer of grace and truth. He is the Lamb of God, that taketh away the sin of the world. Christ is the offer of Christmas. The life that He brings is the real gift God freely offers to the souls of men.

To whom is the gift of Christmas offered? Surely we all know the answer to this question. It is best given in John's words: "For God so loved the world, that he gave his only begotten Son, that whosoever believeth on him should not perish, but have eternal life." The answer is found in the great word 'whosoever'. The Christmas offer is made to every one who will receive Christ. The offer comes to rich and poor, to high and low, to prince and pauper, to men of all races, colors and conditions of life. There is a wideness in God's mercy that embraces the whole world in His proffer of love and grace. God Almighty had no privileged class in mind when He sent His Son! Far from it! He came through the Jewish race but not to the Jewish race exclusively. He came to the Jews and to the Gentiles: to the white men, the black men, the yellow men, the brown men, the red man—in short to all men. God so loved the world that whosoever believeth may in Him have eternal life. "God loves and gives; man believes and lives."

What is the price of God's Christmas offer? One that we all can pay. No one is too poor to take advantage of God's offer. No one can claim that he is too destitute to have Christmas. Some may be denied the many good things that go along with the observance of Christmas, but God will not deny any soul the real Christmas gift if that soul truly wants it. The price is simply that of a heart full of love for God and of faith in the Lord Jesus Christ. In this case, the price itself is provided by the loving Father, and no man is rich enough to buy the gift with money or strong enough to demand it by right of conquest. In fact, God more often brings the blessings of Christmas to the poor and lowly than to them of high degree; more often to the humble cottage than to the proud mansion. The results of Christ's coming as declared in Mary's song continue to appear with each passing generation:

> "He hath put down princes from their thrones,
> And hath exalted them of low degree.
> The hungry he hath filled with good things;
> And the rich he hath sent empty away."

The Saviour of the world was cradled in a lowly manger so that the poor and the humble of all the earth might be able to kneel by His crib and behold the glory of God in His face.

II. The Offer Rejected.

It is recorded in the Gospel and in the national tragedy of a great people that the Christmas offer was at first rejected. Of all sad and poignant words in the New Testament perhaps the saddest are these: "He came unto his own, and they that were his own received him not." The Christmas offer was rejected! The greatest gift ever offered to man was despised! The tenderest love ever poured out in mercy was spurned! How could this be?

People reject attractive Christmas offers for various and sundry reasons. Some feel they do not need the article offered and can get along just as well without it. Some realize they cannot afford even this 'marvelous Christmas bargain'. Some cautious people, who may have good grounds for their scepticism, do not believe the offer to be as good as it is represented. Others may be impressed with the offer and may intend to take advantage of it, but they delay and put off until it is too late. Still others may not pay any attention to this particular offer because they want something else more. A certain number may pass up the offer for the simple reason that they do not like the concern making the offer. And so for one reason or another people reject the commercial offers of the season.

When Jesus came unto His own and they received Him not, there must have been some reason for this rejection. We are not left to guess concerning the reason. There are certain passages in the Gospels which clearly reveal the charges the Jewish officials brought against Jesus. These were mainly two: He broke their Sabbath rules by setting aside their traditions, and called God His Father, making Himself equal with God. Sabbath breaking and blasphemy, these were the accusations of the Jews against Jesus. There are also certain passages which record Jesus' charges against the Jews who rejected Him. Jesus charged them with not knowing the Father and not having the love of God in their hearts. Another charge was that they did not know or believe their own Scriptures. Still another was that they were walking in moral blindness and hence could not see the true light when it shone in their midst. On one occasion "Jesus said unto them, If God were your Father, ye would love me: for I came forth and am come from God; for neither have I come of myself, but he sent me." But they did not hear His voice and did not follow Him. They did not know the Good Shepherd because they were not of His sheep. The Door stood open, but they would not enter in.

Why are so many people rejecting God's Christmas offer to-day? We scarcely need to affirm the truth that multitudes of people are rejecting Christ and the way of life He requires of His followers. The condemnatory words of John the Baptist are just as true to-day as they were when he hurled them forth to the unbelieving Jews beside the Jordan: "In the midst of you standeth one whom ye know not." Multitudes of people to-day do not know Christ as their personal Saviour and apparently do not care to know Him in this sense. We may think there are many reasons why people continue to reject Christ as Saviour and Lord, but all of them may be reduced to two: religious and moral. Those who reject Christ to-day do not know the Father nor have the love of God in themselves; secondly, they are walking in moral darkness and evil. Two things are necessary for all such unbelievers to secure salvation, namely, repentance toward God and faith toward Jesus Christ. The reasons for men's indifference to Christ, the Kingdom and the Church are not superficial and negligible, they are profound and fundamental. Men are in the habit of giving all kinds of excuses for their indifferences and neglect, and of directing all kinds of criticism against the Church and Christianity. But when all is said and done, we may be sure that Christ is rejected to-day, as in all the past, by those who do not love God and do not want to walk in the light of the holy and sacrificial life of Christ. Men do not accept the Christmas offer because they have no love for the One Who makes the offer, and because they do not feel the need of the new life the Gift of God will bring to them.

III. The Offer Accepted.

It is much more pleasing and profitable to dwell upon the rewards that come to those who accept God's Christmas offer. "But as many as received him, to them he gave the right to become children of God." This is the Gospel message in a word: those who accept God's love gift in Christ become the children of God. There is a sense of course in which all men are God's children. God is the

Father of mankind in that He is the Creator and preserver of all who live upon the earth. But there is another sense in which men must become the children of God, namely, by coming to know God the Father through His Son, the Lord Jesus Christ. Men must acknowledge Christ as their Redeemer and Saviour in order to become true children of God.

This takes us to the very heart of the whole matter. God sent His Son for this very purpose that He might save the world from perishing in its sins. Christ came as the Saviour. "Thou shalt call his name JESUS; for it is he that shall save his people from their sins." "There is born to you this day in the city of David a Saviour, who is Christ the Lord." We become children of God when we receive Christ, believe on His name, and are born anew by the Spirit of God.

In receiving Christ and being united with Him, we become heirs of all the privileges and blessings God has promised to them that love Him. As Paul emphatically puts it: "The Spirit himself beareth witness with our spirit, that we are children of God: and if children, then heirs; heirs of God, and joint-heirs with Christ." To appreciate the blessings we have as children of God we need to take into consideration the whole plan of salvation as it is unfolded to us in the Gospel. Perhaps it can best be summed up for us in the phrase 'eternal life'. Christ came to give eternal life to those who receive Him. "And this is life eternal, that they should know thee the only true God, and him whom thou didst send, even Jesus Christ." John declares that his Gospel was written "that ye may believe that Jesus is the Christ, the Son of God; and that believing ye may have life in his name."

This message is being brought to people to-day who have already accepted Christ and who believe in His name. But it is certainly true that we all need to accept God's offer more fully and to possess more completely the spiritual blessings which belong to us as joint-heirs with Christ. It is also certainly true that the Christmas season should bring us all closer to Christ and make us more conscious of our divine rights as children of God. There is not one who has received the Son of God in the way He is entitled to be received. There is not one who has not been crowding Him out in one way or another. There is not one who cannot provide a warmer, brighter room in his heart for the Christ-child than he has yet done. And so He comes again to offer His grace and truth and love to every heart. What will you do with God's Christmas offer this year? Will the ancient tragedy of rejection be repeated in your life? or will the blessed gift of God's love find a truer welcome than ever before?

We need Christmas more and more with each passing year. We need its simplicity, its reality, its good-will, its hope. We need to hear again the angels' song, to gain a clearer perception of spiritual verities, to rediscover the whole of life in keeping with the message and spirit of Christmas. Our generation is one of sad disillusionment, scepticism, doubt, fear, uncertainty, material mindedness. Like Tennyson's "Lady of Shalott," the earnest people of our generation have grown "half sick of shadows". They yearn for the real, the true, the good. Their souls cry out for certainty, for security, for God. The Christmas offer meets this very need —the deepest need of this generation or any other—the need for God in all of His saving power and keeping love.

The challenge to receive and share the Christmas Offer is admirably expressed by Grace Noll Crowell in a little poem entitled "Let Us Keep Christmas":

> "Whatever else be lost among the years,
> Let us keep Christmas still a shining thing;
> Whatever doubts assail us, or what fears,
> Let us hold close one day, remembering
> Its poignant meaning for the hearts of men.
> Let us get back our childlike faith again.
>
> Wealth may have taken wings, yet still there are
> Clear windowpanes to glow with candlelight;
> There are boughs for garlands, and a tinsel star
> To tip some little fir tree's lifted height.
> There is no heart too heavy or too sad,
> But some small gift of love can make it glad.
>
> And there are home-sweet rooms where laughter rings,
> And we can sing the carols as of old.
> Above the eastern hills a white star swings;
> There is an ancient story to be told;
> There are kind words and cheering words to say.
> Let us be happy on the Christ Child's day."

THE QUIET IN THE LAND

O Little Town of Bethlehem

O little town of Bethlehem,
  How still we see thee lie;
Above thy deep and dreamless sleep
  The silent stars go by:
Yet in thy dark streets shineth
  The everlasting Light;
The hopes and fears of all the years
  Are met in thee to-night.

For Christ is born of Mary;
  And gathered all above,
While mortals sleep, the angels keep
  Their watch of wondering love.
O morning stars, together
  Proclaim the holy birth;
And praises sing to God the King,
  And peace to men on earth.

How silently, how silently
  The wondrous gift is given!
So God imparts to human hearts
  The blessings of His heaven.
No ear may hear His coming,
  But in this world of sin,
Where meek souls will receive Him still,
  The dear Christ enters in.

O holy Child of Bethlehem,
  Descend to us, we pray;
Cast out our sin, and enter in,
  Be born in us to-day.
We hear the Christmas angels
  The great glad tidings tell;
O come to us, abide with us,
  Our Lord Emmanuel.

—BISHOP PHILLIPS BROOKS, 1868

III

The Quiet in the Land

LUKE 1:52, *He hath put down princes from their thrones,*
And hath exalted them of low degree.

I. The Quiet Manner of His Coming.

THE fulness of time has come. The greatest event of human history is about to come to pass. The advent of the Son of God is nigh at hand. How will God send His only begotten Son into the world? What human agencies will He employ in this main act of the drama of redemption? Surely in bringing to pass an event of such momentous significance the Almighty will call into operation new and hitherto unknown creative forces. Surely He will enlist the co-operation of the great and powerful and influential of earth in providing a suitable welcome and reception for His well beloved Son. What does God do? The strange thing is that Christmas came about in the way it did. This is the perennial mystery; this the marvel of marvels; this the beautiful miracle of Christmas.

In our day and generation one of the mightiest nations of earth has conducted a brilliant coronation ceremony for its new king. The whole world knows about the spectacular event. It was a magnificent affair. No cost was spared in making it an occasion of royal splendor, pomp, and glory. The great personages of the empire, the princes and potentates of many nations participated in this coronation ceremony. The news concerning every detail was flashed around the world. Millions of people read the vivid reports in the newspapers. The radio carried the glowing accounts to multitudes of eager listeners in all sections of the earth. This coronation did not take place in a hidden corner!

But what about the birth of Jesus Christ? Did the whole world know of His coming? Were the great ones of earth, the princes, emperors, kings and dignitaries ready to welcome Him and to honor Him as the King of Kings and Lord of Lords? Did God publish abroad the good tidings of the Saviour's birth in the courts and palaces of the crowned-heads; in the pleasure gardens of the wealthy and frivolous; in the halls of learning and philosophy; in the temples of religion; in the armed camps of mighty warriors? How strange, how passing strange, that God should work in such unnatural ways; in such direct contrast with time-honored worldly methods! How strange that He should sweep aside all of the pomp and glory of earth and introduce heaven's unknown simplicity in bringing to pass the greatest event of all time!

II. The Quiet Souls Who Received Him.

Let us consider the social structure of the age and land into which Jesus was born. The Roman Empire held Palestine in its mighty grip. The Jews were a subject people. They had their kings and rulers, but these were shorn of all real power. The New Testament gives us a clear picture of the social structure of the Jewish nation. The Pharisees were the dominant party. They were ardent patriots, bitterly despising the yoke of Rome. They were the religious rulers of the time, the party that gave the distinctive coloring to the religious life of the nation. They were religious formalists, zealous, scrupulous, exacting, but lacking the real spiritual essence of religion. The Pharisees, numbering a few thousands, belonged to the middle class of people. The Scribes were closely associated with the Pharisees in religious matters. They were the interpreters of the Scriptures, the teachers in the synagogues, the lawyers of the people. They professed unbounded reverence for every word and letter of the Scriptures, but they were enslaved to a dead system of rules and rituals that were a burden to themselves and to the people. In their system of handling the Scriptures the ceremonial and traditional had entirely displaced the moral and spiritual. Their application of the laws of Moses invariably overlooked the spiritual, vital, human and divine elements which their Scriptures contained. The Sadducees were the liberals and rationalists in religion. They were sceptical, cold-hearted, worldly men who belonged for the most part to the upper and wealthy classes, to the courtly party. They opposed the Pharisees in their strict interpretations of the Law, and were famous for their denial of the resurrection. They had nothing of religious warmth or fervor to give the people. They, as well as the Scribes and Pharisees, were blind leaders of the blind. Then there was the lower class of people comprised of the country people, the laboring classes, the poor and humble. At the bottom of society were the outcasts, publicans, harlots, and sinners who were despised, neglected and abused even by the religious leaders of the nation.

James Stalker, in his book, "The Trial and Death of Jesus Christ," gives this picture of the nation: "The age was spiritually dead. Religion was represented by the high-and-dry formalism of the Pharisees on the one hand and the cold and worldly scepticism of the Sadducees on the other. In the synagogues the people asked for bread and were offered a stone. The scribes, instead of letting the pure river of Bible truth flow over the land, choked up its course with the sand of their soulless commentary. Yet there are good people even in the worst of times. There were truly pious souls sprinkled up and down Palestine. They were like lights shining here and there, at great intervals, in the darkness. They could not but feel that they were strangers and foreigners in their own age and country, and they lived in the past and the future. The prophets, on whose words they nourished their souls, foretold a good time coming, when on those who sat in darkness there would burst a great light. For this better time, then, they were waiting. They were waiting to hear the voice of prophecy echoing once more through the land and waking the population from its spiritual slumber. They were waiting, above all, for the Messiah, if they might dare to hope that He would come in their days."

As we read the Nativity chapters in Matthew and Luke we come into intimate relationship with the human actors in the Christmas drama. Who are these pious souls whom God selected to introduce His Gift of Love to the world? Harris Franklin Rall, in his excellent little book, "The Life of Jesus," has this to say: "We should be grateful for these first pages of Luke because of the picture that they give us of a circle that we might not otherwise know. The New Testament shows us the Pharisees, but they were only a few thousand; it shows us the Sadducees, but of these there were still less. But it shows us this other circle too, the simple, devout souls like Zacharias and Elisabeth, Joseph and Mary, the shepherds, and Simeon and Anna. You cannot tell the real life of a nation by what you read of its 'prominent people', or by the names and tales that figure in newspaper headlines. In these quiet souls was the real heart of Israel; here its deepest faith and devotion lived on; they have been called 'the quiet in the land.' As we study these songs of Zacharias and Mary, we note how these folks fed not so much upon the traditions of the law as upon the words of psalmist and prophet. Later we find Jesus drawing inspiration from these same sources. These folks did not teach the people, as did the scribes; nor govern the nation, as did the priests. But they had a higher glory and wrought greater service: they furnished the homes in which were born and nurtured John the Baptist and Jesus of Nazareth."

The quiet in the land! These then were the true people of God through whom the greatest event of all time came to fulfilment. These humble, pious souls were the first to receive the Son of God into their hearts and lives. These were the quiet, unknown and unnoticed people whom God used to bless the world with the good tidings of the Saviour's birth. He "hath exalted them of low degree!" Concerning Zacharias and Elisabeth it is written: "And they were both righteous before God, walking in all the commandments and ordinances of the Lord blameless." These were the godly parents whose religious faith and life nurtured the soul of John the Baptist, the Forerunner of Christ. The venerable priest's benediction is full of fatherly tenderness:

> "Yea and thou, child, shalt be called the prophet of the Most High:
> For thou shalt go before the face of the Lord to make ready his
>   ways;
> To give knowledge of salvation unto his people
> In the remission of their sins."

Concerning Mary, the mother of Jesus, it is written: "Hail, thou that art highly favored, the Lord is with thee." Mary's meek and obedient spirit is seen in her reply: "And Mary said, Behold, the handmaid of the Lord; be it unto me according to thy word." Her song of praise and adoration expresses the deep spiritual exultation that filled her soul; it is a song of pure praise to God for His goodness and mercy to her and through her to His people. Her penetrating insight, enlivened by the Holy Spirit, enabled her to affirm the wonderful truth of the Christmas miracle and mystery:

> "He hath put down princes from their thrones,
> *And hath exalted them of low degree.*"

The genuine piety of these quiet souls is seen throughout the Scripture story in their prompt obedience to the word of God as brought to them by His angelic-messengers. It is reflected in the songs of praise which poured from their pure hearts filled with the promises of God to His people in His written Word. It is seen in their faithful observance of the religious rites enjoined upon them by the Law of Moses. They kept the law of circumcision; they observed the law of purification; they attended the feast of the passover every year in the temple of Jerusalem. The statements concerning the childhood of John and of Jesus are tributes to the religious piety of the homes in which they grew up. We should always keep this fact in mind when we read the words concerning Jesus: "And the child grew, and waxed strong, filled with wisdom: and the grace of God was upon him." Again, "And Jesus advanced in wisdom and stature, and in favor with God and men." The quiet in the land fulfilled in themselves the prophet Micah's conception of true religion: "And what doth Jehovah require of thee, but to do justly, and to love kindness, and to walk humbly with thy God?" Their conception of the national mission of Israel exalted moral and religious values as the true glory of the people of God. The devout priest Zacharias longed for the time when the nation should return to God and

"Should serve him without fear,
In holiness and righteousness before him all our days."

III. The Quiet Keepers of the Faith.

The message for our day and generation is so plain that he that runs may read. The quiet in the land are always honored and exalted by being called to become co-workers with God. They are always the light of the world and the salt of the earth. They are always the hope of the nation and the harbingers of a better day for the world. It was true in the beginning, and it has been true down through the history of the Church. W. T. Hanzsche, in his splendid volume, "The Presbyterians," has pointed out this same truth. He says, "It is really amazing that Christianity continued at all through the Dark Ages in the face of the pagan barbarian hordes, and the later invasion of Europe by the Mohammedan Turks. God seemed to nest the Christian faith in a few quiet lives, and nurture it in a few out-of-the-way places through the long, dark years which form the Middle Ages." Robert Burns, in his justly famous poem, "The Cotter's Saturday Night," gives us a winsome picture of piety in one of the humble homes of Scotland. After describing the devout manner in which the cotter and his family fed their souls upon the Word of God and offered prayer to God for His continued goodness and care, the poet-prophet affirms:

> "From scenes like these, old Scotia's grandeur springs,
> That makes her lov'd at home, rever'd abroad."

What about our nation and time? Wherein lies the hope of our nation if not in the humble homes and in the pious lives of the true people of God? And yet multitudes of our people have been looking to other means and methods for their salvation. They have been looking to political leaders, to governmental remedies, to economic panaceas for their hope of prosperity and well being in the future. Even at Christmas time, when spiritual values should be uppermost in the minds of the people, the land is inundated by a tidal wave of commercial activity and materialistic self-seeking that quite obliterates the quiet, peaceful, spiritual meaning of the birth of Jesus Christ. A nation of people will never discover the resources of salvation and abundant life in Jesus Christ for themselves and for the world by continuing the observance of Christmas on this basis. We must recapture the spirit and the piety of the quiet in the land; the devout fervor of those rare souls who were the first to share the joy and blessing of His coming. If we are to know the meaning of Christmas, and share its meaning with others, nothing else than a humble, faithful walk of fellowship with God in Christ will do. The spiritual law of Christ's kingdom abides for ever: "And whosoever shalt exalt himself shall be humbled; and whosoever shall humble himself shall be exalted." We should believe in the possibility and rejoice in the opportunity that we may be numbered among the quiet in the land. The message of the angels is for the everlasting present: "There is born to *you — this day —* a Saviour, who is Christ the Lord." It is still true for the quiet in all lands that

> "No ear may hear His coming,
> But in this world of sin,
> Where meek souls will receive Him still,
> The dear Christ enters in."

THE CHRISTMAS STAR

Brightest and Best of the Sons of the Morning

Brightest and best of the sons of the morning,
  Dawn on our darkness, and lend us thine aid;
Star of the east, the horizon adorning,
  Guide where our infant Redeemer is laid.

Cold on His cradle the dewdrops are shining;
  Low lies His head with the beasts of the stall:
Angels adore Him in slumber reclining,
  Maker and Monarch and Saviour of all.

Say, shall we yield Him, in costly devotion,
  Odors of Edom and offerings Divine,
Gems of the mountain and pearls of the ocean,
  Myrrh from the forest, or gold from the mine?

Vainly we offer each ample oblation;
  Vainly with gifts would His favor secure:
Richer by far is the heart's adoration;
  Dearer to God are the prayers of the poor.

Brightest and best of the sons of the morning,
  Dawn on our darkness, and lend us thine aid;
Star of the east, the horizon adorning,
  Guide where our infant Redeemer is laid.
                              —Bishop Reginald Heber, 1811

IV

The Christmas Star

MATTHEW 2:2, *Where is he that is born King of the Jews? for we saw his star in the east, and are come to worship him.*

"THERE shall come forth a star out of Jacob," cried Balaam the son of Beor, as he foretold the coming of Israel's sceptred King in the dim, distant future. The centuries of prophetic insight, ever growing clearer and more distant, rolled by. Who would be the first to see the Bright and Morning Star? Isaiah's prophecy seems to have contained the truth regarding the watchers of the Gentile world. Said he: "And nations shall come to thy light, and kings to the brightness of thy rising." And so it came to pass that Wise-men from the east were the first to behold "his star" in their own night sky and eventually to follow its guiding beacon within the borders of Israel.

The Christmas Star has a manifold meaning for humanity. "The hopes and fears of all the years" are centered in that Star. It has a meaning for each individual according to the spiritual insight and personal needs of that individual. It is ever a symbol of humanity's highest hopes and spiritual aspirations. To many it is the shining emblem of life's Ideal, whatever that ideal may be. Again, it will continue to stand as the harbinger of a brighter day for the world when peace shall heal the wounds of war, and good will shall bind the hearts of men into a brotherhood of nations. Whatever incidental meaning the Christmas Star may have, its central meaning should be held fast by all those upon whose hearts the true Light has shined. The Star of Jacob is Christ—the Son of God; the Son of man; the Saviour of the world. He is the Star of supreme glory; the brightest Star in the firmament of God's love. He is humanity's highest Ideal; most inspiring Hope, most enduring Reward. The noblest quest to which an individual soul can be devoted is to follow the light of His Star; the highest goal toward which humanity can move in its onward struggle for righteousness, truth and freedom is the goal of His dream for a redeemed, sanctified, glorified race of men.

I. The Star Risen.

There are those who consider the Star of the East as an astronomical phenomenon and who affirm that they can affix the precise date of its appearing. These would explain its appearing as a merely natural phenomenon. Others regard it as a supernatural event; a special sign in the accepted Biblical sense granted by Almighty God to accompany the greatest event of all time, the birth of Jesus Christ, the Son of God. This is the only satisfactory view to hold; the only suitable explanation that accords with the other glorious facts of His Nativity. But we are concerned primarily with the rising of the Star as a spiritual fact, and as such it holds an abiding meaning for all of the generations of men.

There comes a time in the life of each normal human being when the star of spiritual aspiration rises in the Orient sky. It gleams in the darkness of human ignorance and depravity with a divine fire. It shines in upon our hearts as an ideal to follow. It calls us to rise up and face the light. It troubles our sinful complacency as with a divine spark. It summons us to undertake the quest of life. It beckons us on to the particular destiny that the Creator of the Star and the Maker of Man has marked out for each one. The Star appears at different times, in various ways, and under widely differing circumstances. But its effect is always the same. It appears as the symbol of hope, aspiration, promise, fulfilment. It summons all who behold its rising to undertake the quest of eternal life.

Those favored students of the starry hosts in the long ago would well remember the night when the star of incomparable glory dawned upon their wondering eyes. Its appearing marked a distinct crisis in their lives. To their eager minds and reverent hearts it brought the light of the glory of God and the answer to the mystery of life and the universe. We do well to recall our own individual experience of the dawning light. It may have been gradual, it may have been sudden, it may have been climactic. But when the star appeared we knew that God was speaking to our souls.

II. The Star Followed.

The Wise-men saw "his star" in the east, but the quest to which it summoned them led them to the far-distant west. It was not an easy matter for them to undertake the journey. It involved the breaking up of their ordinary, routine life. It necessitated careful and costly preparation for a long, difficult and perilous journey. It carried them forward to a great adventure in unknown lands and among strange peoples. It was a quest to try the stoutest of hearts and the bravest of spirits. It is quite possible, as Henry van Dyke suggests in his story of "The Other Wise Man," that there were others who likewise saw the star in the east, but who were too faint-hearted to undertake the quest. Those who did follow the star were hardy pioneer souls, brave knights of daring emprise, loyal searchers of the priceless truth. Whatever their age may have been, they possessed the spirit, vision and faith of eternal youth. They were ready to follow the star even though it entailed self-denial, hardship and unknown trials.

All who follow the light of the wandering star must be prepared to sacrifice personal ease, comfort and security in order to attain their goal. Inevitably there must be the break with the old life, old associations, old companions. The student must leave his home and family and spend a number of years in preparation for his life work. The scientific explorer must go to the frigid ends of the earth and risk his life in the terrible loneliness of the dread Antarctic night in order to carry out his investigations. In the early days, the pioneer foreign missionaries who left the shores of America for the darkness of heathen lands expected never to return! The prophet must leave his sheepfold, his plow or his sycamore trees and go where the voice of God sends him. The disciple must leave his fishing-nets or his place of toll and rise up and follow wheresoever the Master leads. All who have tried to follow the star-lit trails of life can bear witness from their own experience to the truth of Jesus' words: "If any man would come after me, let him deny himself, and take up his cross, and follow me."

III. The Star Lost.

The Wise-men who saw the rising of Messiah's star did not have the star to guide them continuously to their journey's end. The holy quest to which they were called was not as simple as that.

To be sure, they had the memory of that celestial light. But they were compelled to travel many days and nights, over many weary miles of deserts and mountains, without the presence of the Shepherd Star to guide them. The star was lost for the time being, but they were to recover it again. They could journey on in hope and assurance because they knew they had seen the star and because they believed Him to be faithful Who had promised. It is always better to have seen the star and lost it than never to have seen it at all.

Temple Bailey, in her beautiful Christmas story, "The Star in the Well," recounts the legend concerning the Well of the Magi. The pious old grandmother in the story is speaking: "I heard it when I was in the Holy Land. They showed me the Well of the Magi. And they said when the Wise Men were traveling towards Bethlehem with the Star guiding them that the morning came and the stars were blotted out by the dawning light, even the great Star which they had followed. And the Wise Men wandered on their way, weary and wondering what they should do. And at last they came to a well and stopped to drink. The waters of the well were deep and dark, and as the first Wise man bent above them he saw mirrored in the deep, dark waters the Star they had lost. And he called to the others and they bent and looked, and behold, there was the Star!"

The lost Star! How many unbelieving, disillusioned, bewildered, unhappy people there are in this world of ours who have lost the Star! The star of faith is lost to many, even in the circles of higher learning; the star of spiritual aspiration is lost to multitudes of young and old who have given themselves over to the pursuit of sordid materialism and carnal pleasures; the star of peace is lost to the struggling millions who are the victims of merciless war; the star of hope is lost to masses of weary people who have succumbed to the burdens, cares and sorrows of life. But the Star is still there! It is still shining from everlasting to everlasting. The world has lost it because it has stopped looking for the Star and has fallen to grovelling in the mire. One glorious star-lit night I observed that when I stood beneath a glaring street-lamp and tried to see the stars they were all blotted out. My proximity to the glaring lamp-light blotted out entirely for the time being the whole expanse of the starry heavens! The Star of Bethlehem is lost to a world in trouble and sin because its vision is blinded by the glaring lights of man's own evil fashioning.

IV. The Star Recovered.

The Wise-men journeyed to Jerusalem, the great capitol of Judea. They produced consternation throughout the city by saying, "Where is he that is born King of the Jews? for we saw his star in the east, and are come to worship him." Herod the king hastily summoned the chief priests and scribes of the people and inquired of them where the Christ should be born. They turned to their scriptures and read from the prophecy of Micah concerning the Messiah's predicted birth in Bethlehem. But these scribes did not believe their own scriptures! They were dwelling within a few miles of the birthplace of Messiah, but they did not see the Star, neither did they go to worship Him. The people of David's own city were not prepared for the coming of their King!

But the Wise-men from the Gentile world accepted the truth of the Jewish scriptures and eagerly hastened on toward Bethlehem. "And lo, the star, which they saw in the east, went before them, till it came and stood over where the young child was." They were rewarded for their faith and perseverance. They continued their quest despite all barriers and difficulties. They carried on their search until they found the goal for which they were seeking. The glorious star which had long been lost to their view was recovered. They did not lose it again, for it was closer to them than when it had first appeared and it guided them unerringly to the Christ, the Light of the World.

V. The Star Superseded.

What a simple and quiet ending to this historic journey; this life-long quest for the wisdom of life; this arduous search for the secret which lies at the heart of the universe! "And they came into the house and saw the young child with Mary his mother; and they fell down and worshipped him; and opening their treasures they offered unto him gifts, gold and frankincense and myrrh." God had spoken to them in the glory of His created heavens; He had inspired and guided them by His written Word, but He revealed His Fatherhood, eternal love and salvation to them in the person of "the young child," the only begotten Son of God, full of grace and truth.

The Wise-men did not need the star to guide them on their return journey. The star had completed its revealing mission. The star had been superseded by the glory of the Child—the Child Immanuel, God with us. He was none other than the Sun of Righteousness, the Light of Men, the Light of the World. The study of natural science, philosophy, history, the Scriptures, theology— all should lead to Christ and find their fulfilment in Him. He is the Wisdom of the Ages, the Ideal of Humanity, the Purpose of History, the Salvation of the World, the Way, the Truth and the Life. Until all seeking souls find Him, their search is incomplete. But when questing spirits have found Him, they have reached the end of their quest. He that sees Christ, sees the Father. He that knows the only true God, and Jesus Christ the Son, has found eternal life. The Christmas Star is Christ. The Star rises for the believer when he is born again; the faithful disciple follows the Star; he loses the comforting presence of the Star through sin and neglect; he recovers the Star when he returns to the path of obedience; some day the Light which he follows with the eye of faith will be present to his enraptured gaze in glory, and he shall behold the Star of his soul face to face.

THE BIRTH OF JESUS CHRIST

Come, Thou Long-Expected Jesus

Come, Thou long-expected Jesus,
  Born to set Thy people free;
From our fears and sins release us;
  Let us find our rest in Thee.

Israel's Strength and Consolation,
  Hope of all the earth Thou art;
Dear Desire of every nation,
  Joy of every longing heart.

Born Thy people to deliver,
  Born a child, and yet a King,
Born to reign in us for ever,
  Now Thy gracious kingdom bring.

By Thine own eternal Spirit
  Rule in all our hearts alone;
By Thine all-sufficient merit
  Raise us to Thy glorious throne.

—Rev. Charles Wesley, 1744

V

The Birth of Jesus Christ

MATTHEW 1:18, *Now the birth of Jesus Christ was on this wise: When his mother Mary had been betrothed to Joseph, before they came together she was found with child of the Holy Spirit.*

CHRISTMAS is the holy festival commemorative of the birth of Jesus Christ. It is the day set apart by Christendom to mark the anniversary of the most significant birthday in all history. Strange as it may seem, the day we observe as Christmas was not the date of His birth. You and I know the exact dates on which we were born. We know the year and we know the day. Some of us well remember the exact hour and minute when our own children were born. But the exact date of the birth of Jesus Christ is lost in obscurity. There is not even conclusive evidence as to the *year* of His birth! He was not born at the beginning of the year 1 A. D., but probably in the year 5 or 4 B. C. The day of His birth has been assigned to practically every month in the year. One authority states that it was sometime between April and October. Another states that it was sometime between November and March. Alfred Plummer concludes: "December 25th cannot be traced higher than the fourth century, and it seems to have been adopted first in the West. We must be content to remain in ignorance as to the date of the birth of Christ."

It is a sad and humiliating thing to discover that the date of December 25th was selected in the early centuries because it corresponded with the season of a pagan festival, the Roman Saturnalia. But it is even more distressing to realize that a large portion of the modern observance of Christmas is more like the pagan Saturnalia than the holy and sacred festivities which belong to the real Christmas. We observe that the name "Christ" makes up two-thirds of the word "Christmas". This suggests to us that we ought to see to it that the day we observe as Christ's birthday should at least be predominantly Christian, if not wholly devoted to His honor. The most hallowed birthday in all the world is surely worthy of our deepest respect, reverence and homage.

I. The Conception by the Holy Spirit.

Among all them that have been born of women the birth of Jesus Christ is absolutely unique. The manner of His birth is delicately and simply described by Matthew: "She was found with child of the Holy Spirit." Since the third century believers have been affirming this sublime fact in the language of the Apostles' Creed: "I believe . . . in Jesus Christ . . . who was conceived by the Holy Ghost, born of the Virgin Mary." The prophet Isaiah foretold this miraculous conception of the promised Messiah many centuries before it came to pass. "Therefore the Lord himself will give you a sign: behold, a virgin shall conceive, and bear a son, and shall call his name Immanuel." Matthew declares that this prophecy is fulfilled in the birth of Mary's Son.

In the fulness of time, the angel Gabriel appeared to the virgin Mary and said unto her, "Fear not, Mary: for thou hast found favor with God. And behold, thou shalt conceive in thy womb, and bring forth a son, and shalt call his name JESUS." The troubled maiden replied, "How shall this be, seeing I know not a man?" "And the angel answered and said unto her, The Holy Spirit shall come upon thee, and the power of the Most High shall overshadow thee: wherefore also the holy thing which is begotten shall be called the Son of God."

When in the course of those troublous and mysterious days the Virgin-mother finally whispered her secret to her betrothed husband, Joseph, he was overwhelmed with the news. Sorrowfully and kindly, yet nonetheless firmly, he was determined to give Mary a letter of divorce and send her away as privately as possible. "But when he thought on these things, behold, an angel of the Lord appeared unto him in a dream, saying, Joseph, thou son of David, fear not to take unto thee Mary thy wife: for that which is conceived in her is of the Holy Spirit." It is altogether fitting that the birth of the Son of God should have been thus unique. As David Smith remarks, "He was conceived by the operation of the Holy Spirit in the womb of a virgin, a new creation of God's hand, a divine man, a second and greaterAdam." He was the Son of David after the flesh; the Son of God after the Spirit.

It is a grievous thing to recall the blind and bitter controversies that have been waged through the centuries over the doctrine of the Virgin Birth. It is disheartening to know that to many people this beautiful miracle of Divine grace has been nothing more than a stone of stumbling and a rock of offense. Surely it is the part of chastened wisdom and of humble faith to accept this beautiful fact as an integral part of the history of Jesus Christ, along with the other glorious facts of His atoning death, triumphant resurrection, heavenly ascension and His coming again. Those who still belong to an age of doubt and unbelief need a double portion of the humble spirit of the Virgin of Nazareth who said, "Behold, the handmaid of the Lord; be it unto me according to thy word."

II. The Incarnation of the Son of God.

The birth of Jesus Christ is absolutely unique in that His coming into the world did not mark the beginning of life for Him, as our being born into the world marks the beginning of life for us. He lived before He began His earthly life; He existed in another form before He took upon Himself our human nature. Therefore His birth was an Advent. It was the Incarnation of One Who had been from all eternity with the Father in glory.

The Prologue to John's Gospel contains these amazing declarations concerning the pre-existence of Christ: "In the beginning was the Word, and the Word was with God, and the Word was God. The same was in the beginning with God. . . . And the Word became flesh, and dwelt among us(and we beheld his glory, glory as of the only begotten from the Father), full of grace and truth." Paul teaches the same identical truth in the second chapter of his letter to the Philippians. "Have this mind in you, which was also in Christ Jesus: who, existing in the form of God, . . . emptied himself, taking the form of a servant, being made in the likeness of men." Jesus Himself, in His great intercessory prayer, referred to this pre-existent heavenly state with the Father. "And now, Father, glorify thou me with thine own self with the glory which I had with thee before the world was. . . . Father, . . . thou lovedst me before the foundation of the world."

The birth of Jesus Christ differs from all others in that His was an Incarnation and not an ordinary human birth. The Son of God, the Lord of Glory, equal in substance, power and glory with the eternal God took upon Himself our human nature and was made in the likeness of men. He was born of a woman and so possessed our true human nature. But God was His Father, and so in a genuine, unique and complete sense He was the only begotten Son of God. He was Immanuel—God with us in human flesh. He was the God-man, combining in His unique personality the characteristics of perfect manhood and complete Godhood.

Hence His Incarnation was a great act of humiliation. He gave up, for the period of His earthly life, the heavenly glory which He shared with the Father from the foundation of the world and humbled Himself by taking upon Himself our human nature. The language of the New Testament describes this act of humiliation, but it is impossible for the human mind to grasp its full significance. The artist tries to capture on his canvas the glorious colors of the sunset, but how infinitely more beautiful and glorious is the sunset itself than any painting can possibly be! Even so the lowly birth of Jesus in the stable of Bethlehem represents the greatest possible subordination of the true power and glory of the eternal Son of God. Let us remember that He endured this humiliation for us. He took our human nature upon Himself that He might know our frame; that He might bear all of our ills, troubles and sins in His own body; that He might die the death of the cross and save us from sin and death unto eternal life.

III. The Fulfilment of Prophecy.

The birth of Jesus Christ is unique in that it marked the fulfilment of prophecy. This progressive revelation concerning the promised Redeemer was God's way of preparing the world for His coming and His mission. The author of Genesis wrote of the seed of the woman that should bruise the serpent's heel. Moses foretold the time when the Lord God should raise up a prophet like unto himself. Balaam predicted that "a star shall come forth out of Jacob." Isaiah prophesied concerning the Child with the Wonderful Name, the "Shoot out of the stock of Jesse", the virgin-born son Immanuel, the Suffering Servant who "was wounded for our transgressions." Micah predicted the very birthplace of the Messiah.

and described Him as One Who would be the Shepherd of His people Israel. More immediate prophecies were uttered by the angel Gabriel, by Mary the virgin and by Zacharias, the father of John the Baptist. These prophecies were all fulfilled in the birth of Mary's child, the Son of the Most High.

The birth of Christ is thus connected with the history of humanity. His coming is related to all of the past history of God's dealings with His people. He came to fulfil all of the covenants, laws, promises, types, ceremonies and hopes that the God of Abraham, Isaac, Jacob, Moses, David and Isaiah had granted to His people. He came in the fulness of time according to God's eternal purpose and decree. He did not come as a fantastic Messiah, full-panoplied with the habiliments of power and glory, but He was born of a lowly peasant mother who was a descendant of the house of David. He *came up through* the travail, the sorrows, the longings and the hopes of humanity. He did not *come down upon* the wicked world from the battlements of heaven to judge, condemn and destroy. "For God sent not the Son into the world to judge the world; but that the world should be saved through him." "For God so loved the world, that he gave his only begotten Son, that whosoever believeth on him should not perish, but have eternal life." Thanks be to God for the Gospel of His redeeming love and grace!

IV. The Accompaniment of Supernatural Signs.

The birth of Jesus Christ is absolutely unique with respect to the supernatural signs that accompanied His advent. We hold that no one can fully appreciate the meaning and beauty of Christmas until he accepts all of these supernatural events as true acts of God and seeks to apprehend the messages of spiritual truth they are intended to convey to believing hearts. Few indeed are they who know the meaning of Christmas in this complete sense! But our aim should be to enrich our experience with these Divine mysteries as each succeeding Christmas comes and goes.

The striking thing to be noted is that all of these accompanying signs were of a quiet, unostentatious, private and deeply spiritual character. The pronouncement to Zacharias concerning the birth of John; the angelic annunciation to Mary; the spiritual rapture of Elisabeth; the heaven-taught wisdom granted to Joseph; the angel herald and the angel chorus heard by the shepherds; the star in the east seen by the Wise-men, and the Spirit-filled utterances of Simeon and Anna—these all belong to the sanctuary of the temple, the privacy of the home, and the seclusion of starlit places. These wonderful signs were not given to the noisy world in general, but to the quiet, waiting hearts of those who were prepared to receive them. Be still, and know that I am God!

V. The Gospel of Salvation.

The birth of Jesus Christ gives to the world the only Gospel of full, free and complete salvation. "And thou shalt call his name JESUS; for it is he that shall save his people from their sins." His name, His wonderful name, His name JESUS, the Saviour, Christ the Lord! "His name shall be called Wonderful, Counsellor, Mighty God, Everlasting Father, Prince of Peace." "And in none other is there salvation: for neither is there any other name under heaven, that is given among men, wherein we must be saved." "Wherefore also God highly exalted him, and gave unto him the name which is above every name; that in the name of JESUS every knee should bow, of things in heaven and things on earth and things under the earth, and that every tongue should confess that Jesus Christ is Lord, to the glory of God the Father."

> "At the name of Jesus bowing,
>   Falling prostrate at His feet,
>   King of kings in Heav'n we'll crown Him,
>   When our journey is complete."

VI. The Fact of Spiritual Experience.

The birth of Jesus Christ is an established fact of history. It is the *central* fact of history; the water-shed of the centuries. The birth of Christ fulfilled the Divine purposes of the deep past; ushered in the new world of the long future, and assured the consummation of God's Kingdom.

But the birth of Jesus Christ must become a fact of spiritual experience before our individual lives can benefit from this great act of God's redeeming love. The Old English Carol suggests a great truth:

> "Though Christ a thousand times in Bethlehem be born,
>   And not within thyself, thy soul will be forlorn."

In order to realize the blessing of Christmas, Christ must be born anew in our own hearts. We must receive Him by faith and thus enter into our heritage as the children of God. When Christ is truly born in us we are born again, born from above, born by the will and power of God. This re-birth makes us new creatures in Christ Jesus; the old things are passed away; behold, they are become new. As we abide in Christ and as He abides in us we come to possess more and more of Him and He comes to possess more and more of us. His possession of us and our possession of Him is our hope of glory. For the Son of God Who left His throne in glory to be born into the world as Mary's Child, later promised His disciples that they should share His heavenly glory and reign with Him for ever and ever. To make room in our hearts for the Christ of Christmas is to have Him make room for us in His mansions of glory. Can any one afford to crowd Him out?

PART TWO

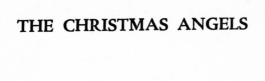

THE CHRISTMAS ANGELS

It Came Upon the Midnight Clear

It came upon the midnight clear,
　　That glorious song of old,
From angels bending near the earth
　　To touch their harps of gold:
"Peace on the earth, good will to men,
　　From heaven's all-gracious King:"
The world in solemn stillness lay,
　　To hear the angels sing.

Still through the cloven skies they come,
　　With peaceful wings unfurled,
And still their heavenly music floats
　　O'er all the weary world:
Above its sad and lowly plains
　　They bend on hovering wing,
And ever o'er its Babel-sounds
　　The blessed angels sing.

And ye, beneath life's crushing load,
　　Whose forms are bending low,
Who toil along the climbing way
　　With painful steps and slow,—
Look now! for glad and golden hours
　　Come swiftly on the wing:
O rest beside the weary road,
　　And hear the angels sing.

For lo, the days are hastening on,
　　By prophet bards foretold,
When with the ever-circling years
　　Comes round the age of gold;
When peace shall over all the earth
　　Its ancient splendors fling,
And the whole world give back the song
　　Which now the angels sing.

　　　　—Rev. Edmund H. Sears, 1850.

VI

The Christmas Angels

PSALM 91:11, *For he will give his angels charge over thee, To keep thee in all thy ways.*

IT MAY seem to be a somewhat risky and altogether futile procedure to speak about angels in this super-sophisticated day of stark realism. In some quarters any serious discussion of the subject would be considered an insult to modern intelligence. A generation of novelty-seeking men and women who worship the "candid camera" and whose intellectual bent is towards the pictorial realism of "Look" and "Life" is not likely to have a very keen appreciation of those unseen celestial beings called angels. However, there is a vast difference between "realism" and "reality". Hence, witnesses of the eternal Word of God may be pardoned for their inflexible purpose to cleave to the eternally real.

We discover that angels occupy a very prominent place in the Bible, in both the Old and New Testaments. They are mentioned in the first and last books of the Bible. They are mentioned in the Historical and Prophetical books of the Old Testament as well as in the Poetical books; in the Gospels and Acts of the Apostles as well as in the Epistles. We read that the angel of the Lord appeared in human form to Abraham, Hagar and Lot; to Moses and Joshua; to Gideon and Manoah. An angel came to Elijah and to Daniel. An angel also aided Peter in his escape from prison and stood by Paul in his time of need. It is quite natural that angels should be especially prominent in the history of Jesus Christ. Angels announced beforehand the birth of John the Forerunner and of Jesus. Angels heralded the good tidings of Jesus' birth to the shepherds. Angels ministered to the needs of the spent Saviour after the Temptation in the Wilderness and the Agony in the Garden. Angels brought tidings to the disciples at the Resurrection and the Ascension. Christ's earthly history begins and closes with the attending ministries of God's holy angels.

In Biblical terminology an angel is a celestial being a little higher in dignity than man. The Psalmist says that man was made a little lower than the angels. As to their nature they are spiritual beings, partaking of the nature of God. In Job they are called "sons of God." They neither marry nor are given in marriage. They are holy in character. Their office is that of messengers of God sent to do His holy will. They differ in rank and dignity, for some are ordinary angels and others are archangels. The angel of the Annunciation is named Gabriel, and Jude refers to Michael the archangel. These unseen yet ever present messengers of God are said to encamp round about them that fear God for the purpose of protecting and delivering them.

The Christmas Angels are undoubtedly the best known of all, for it is at Christmas time that we are most conscious of their existence and most willing to believe in their beneficent care. The angels of Christmas do not all perform the same function or bear the same message. When we consider their combined ministrations in connection with the Redeemer's birth we discover a new wealth of spiritual truth that enriches the total meaning and mystery of Christmas.

I. The Angel of Blessing.

We may think of the Annunciation angel as the Angel of Blessing. This angel, Gabriel, was sent from God to the virgin Mary with a message such as no other woman has ever heard. "Thou . . . art highly favored, the Lord is with thee . . . Thou hast found favor with God . . . The Holy Spirit shall come upon thee." Such was the pronouncement of Divine blessing upon Mary of Nazareth. Later, when Mary went to visit her kinswoman Elisabeth, that godly mother likewise bestowed a unique blessing upon Mary. Filled with the Holy Spirit, she cried out with a loud voice: "Blessed art thou among women, . . . And blessed is she that believed; for there shall be a fulfilment of the things which have been spoken to her from the Lord." Whereupon the mother of the Lord, in a mood of intense spiritual exultation, dwelt upon the same high note in her song, saying, "For behold, from henceforth all generations shall call me blessed."

Mary's prophecy has been fulfilled, for all succeeding generations have regarded her as the most blessed among women. The Church has held her name in highest veneration and reverence. This veneration has been carried to unwarranted extremes by those who practice Mariolatry, who worship her as the Mother of God. This is wrong. Christ alone has been given the name which is above every name. He is to be worshipped as God, but not His mother Mary. She trusted in Him as her Saviour as did the other disciples. Let us regard her as the most blessed among women in being chosen to become the mother of Jesus Christ, but let us do what the Wise-men did when they came into the house and saw the young child with Mary his mother—let us bow down and worship HIM and bestow our gifts upon HIM.

We cannot fail to remark that the bestowal of highest blessing upon Mary carried with it the condition of deepest suffering. Mary seemed to sense this at the time the angel first spoke to her, for she was greatly troubled in her spirit. The venerable Simeon predicted the trial of suffering through which she must pass when he spoke to her in the Temple: "Behold, this child is set for the falling and rising of many in Israel; and for a sign which is spoken against; yea and a sword shall pierce through thine own soul; that thoughts out of many hearts may be revealed." Mary's sufferings began in an unusual way at His birth and were brought to a terrible climax at His death upon the cross. Then, above all other times, the sword of bitter anguish pierced through her own soul.

In God's plan of life for His servants the highest blessing inevitably involves the deepest suffering. God's best gifts to mankind cost the greatest amount of sacrifice, suffering and love. "Greater love hath no man than this, that a man lay down his life for his friends." The greatest love, which is the greatest good, always involves the laying down of life. God so loved that He gave His own Son. Hence, the joy and blessing and happiness we possess in loving the children God has given us have their counterparts of sacrifice, sorrow and suffering. Heaven's highest blessings have their price!

II. The Angel of Duty.

We may think of the angel of the Lord that appeared to Joseph as the Angel of Duty. When Joseph finally learned Mary's secret he was deeply troubled and sorely perplexed. At first, only one course of action seemed possible to him. Although it broke his heart to think of sending his beloved Mary away, yet to his just and righteous mind there seemed to be no other solution to his dark problem. As he lay on his tear-stained pillow turning the matter over and over again in his mind he fell asleep, and "Behold, an angel of the Lord appeared unto him in a dream, saying, Joseph, thou son of David, fear not to take unto thee Mary thy wife." And when he awoke from his sleep he knew what he would do.

This angelic revelation was to Joseph the clear call of duty. He was directed to a definite course of action. This action was in direct contrast with the course he had intended to pursue. His own wisdom had failed him. God knew best. God had shown him the way and he would walk in it. How grateful he was that the God of Israel continued to order the steps of His servants! His mind was at rest. God had called him to the high office of being the Guardian and Protector of His infant Son!

God's people still have their times of perplexity; their grave and difficult problems to solve. Often the way is dark; the visibility is nil; the ceiling is zero. But the instrument board still shows the true course! Keep the ship on her beam and all will be well! The way out of perplexity is to do our duty. The call of duty will frequently clash with the thing we want to do. But we must heed the call of duty at all costs; we must do what we know to be right. God continues to speak of His servants through these simple reminders of plain and lowly tasks. If we are obedient to the heavenly vision, our God will lead us onward in the path of safety, blessing and peace.

III. The Angel of Good Tidings.

We may think of the herald angel that appeared to the shepherds as the Angel of Good Tidings. His message was, "Be not afraid; for behold, I bring you good tidings of great joy which shall be to all the people: for there is born to you this day in the city of David a Saviour, who is Christ the Lord." Milton's description of the event in his poem "Paradise Regained" is impressive. The mother is represented as speaking to her Son:

> "At thy nativity a glorious quire
> Of Angels, in the fields of Bethlehem, sung
> To shepherds, watching at their folds by night

And told them the Messiah now was born,
Where they might see him; and to thee they came,
Directed to the manger where thou lay'st;
For in the inn was left no better room."

The good tidings of the Christmas Angel is a *personal* message. "There is born *to you.*" Each one of us who makes room in his heart for the Saviour has the right to claim God's promised blessings in the gift of His Son. *Whosoever* believeth on Him shall have eternal life. The gift of salvation is within the reach of each one, however high or low, rich or poor, wise or simple. But each must exercise his own gift of faith. Each must open the door of his own heart to let Christ come in.

The good tidings of the Herald Angel is a *present* message. "There is born to you *this day.*" "Now is the acceptable time; behold, now is the day of salvation." "Now is salvation nearer to us than when we first believed." God's separate emphasis is upon the "now"; the eternal present. His salvation keeps ever abreast of human needs; of personal needs and social needs. Christmas is not a day on the calendar; it is a fact of spiritual experience. Christmas Day comes and goes before we know it. But every day may be a day of Christ's new-born salvation; a day of His unfailing presence with us. The needs of to-morrow cannot be supplied with the resources of to-day. Each day, each hour we must depend upon the angel of His presence to save us and keep us.

IV. The Angels of Song.

We naturally think of the heavenly choir of angels as the Angels of Song. What favored men the shepherds were to have had the privilege of hearing their rapturous strains! Surely no sweeter music ever fell upon mortal ears. The author of Job spoke of the gladness of heaven at the time of creation

"When the morning stars sang together,
And all the sons of God shouted for joy."

But the song of the angelic host at the time of the Saviour's birth was a truer and more significant paean of joy. For the song came in the darkest midnight of human need, and it swelled forth with the full tide of hope and salvation.

The song of the angels is primarily a song of praise to God. "Glory to God in the highest" is the dominant note. Christmas is

God-centered; God first thought of Christmas; He so loved us that He sent His Son to be the propitiation for our sins. We are to give God all praise and honor and glory and blessing for the gift of His well beloved Son and for the fulness of salvation provided in Jesus Christ, the Lamb of God.

The song of the angels is a song of peace to men. How slow the world has been to learn the lessons that belong to its peace! How sadly the world stands in need of the heavenly gift of peace to heal its hurts, hatreds and war-weariness! The timely poem of Grace Noll Crowell entitled "On Earth Peace" proclaims the ancient appeal in terms of present day need.

> "How dare men mock the white-robed winging choir!
> How dare they climb the star-lit heavenly lanes
> To loose upon mankind the scarlet fire
> Of Hell itself from roaring battle planes!
> How dare they kill and maim and blind their brothers,
> Forgetting the Christ, the earnest words He said:
> 'Inasmuch as ye have done it unto others,
> Ye have done it unto me . . . ' His heart has bled
> And he is there—one with the hurt and dying,
> Moving among them, waiting for war to cease.
> Hark! The Song above the bitter crying:
> 'Glory to God in the highest—on earth peace.'
> How we have failed Thee, blessed Lord and Master!
> We stand before Thy judgment stricken, dumb,
> God, God help mankind learn its lessons faster,
> And even yet, Lord, may Thy Kingdom come."

V. The Angel of Protection.

Finally, we may think of the angel that appeared to Joseph in Bethlehem and in Egypt as the Angel of Protection. This guardian angel watched over the Holy Family and delivered them from the evil designs of the wicked Herod; he brought them in safety into the land of Egypt; he directed their course on the return journey and led them to their safe retreat in Nazareth of Galilee. Surely the word of the Psalmist was graciously fulfilled in the case of Joseph, Mary and the Infant Saviour:

> "For he will give his angels charge over thee,
> To keep thee in all thy ways.
> They shall bear thee up in their hands,
> Lest thou dash thy foot against a stone."

Do we believe in the protecting care of God's holy angels? Do we really trust in God's promise that "The angel of the Lord encampeth round about them that fear him, and delivereth them?" You and I have never seen an angel. But we have seen their influence and work. Some will say, "Seeing is believing." But we have never seen the force of gravity, and yet we believe in its beneficent power. We have never seen electricity, and yet we use it for all sorts of helpful purposes. We cannot see nor explain love, but we know its redeeming, transforming, ennobling power in human life. In the spiritual realm the word of Jesus to Martha is for ever true: "Said I not unto thee, that, if thou believedst, thou shouldest see the glory of God?" Strange as it may seem to our doubting, disbelieving age, in the spiritual realm the rule is reversed: "Believing is seeing." Those who believe in the angels of God will readily see the effects of their gracious care and keeping in their own lives and in the world.

Christians, Behold! The Holy Spirit, Whom we have not seen, is He not real? Is He not a Person? Is He not Christ with us? The Holy Spirit is our Angel of Blessing, conferring all spiritual blessings upon us. He is our Angel of Duty, guiding us in the perception of duty and strengthening us in the performance of duty. He is our Angel of Good Tidings, taking of the things of Christ and declaring them to us as we are able to receive them. He is our Angel of Song, giving us a song of hope in our hearts even in the midnight of our deepest need. He is our Angel of Protection, fulfilling the comforting words of Him that said, "Lo, I am with you always, even unto the end of the world."

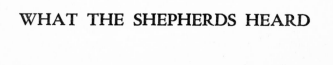

WHAT THE SHEPHERDS HEARD

While Shepherds Watched Their Flocks By Night

While shepherds watched their flocks by night,
    All seated on the ground,
The angel of the Lord came down,
    And glory shone around.

"Fear not," said he,—for mighty dread
    Had seized their troubled mind,—
"Glad tidings of great joy I bring
    To you and all mankind.

"To you, in David's town this day,
    Is born of David's line,
A Saviour, who is Christ the Lord,
    And this shall be the sign:

"'The heavenly Babe you there shall find
    To human view displayed,
All meanly wrapt in swathing bands,
    And in a manger laid."

Thus spake the seraph, and forthwith
    Appeared a shining throng
Of angels praising God, and thus
    Addressed their joyful song:

"All glory be to God on high,
    And to the earth be peace:
Good-will henceforth, from heaven to men,
    Begin and never cease."

—NAHUM TATE, 1702.

VII

What the Shepherds Heard

LUKE 2:10-11, *And the angel said unto them, Be not afraid; for behold, I bring you good tidings of great joy which shall be to all the people: for there is born to you this day in the city of David a Saviour, who is Christ the Lord.*

S T. LUKE'S account of the birth of Jesus includes the story of the shepherds who were the first visitors to see the Holy Child. Luke alone records the visit of the shepherds, while Matthew alone records the visit of the Wise-men. Luke's Gospel is the Gospel of Humanity, and this humble scene of the lowly shepherds kneeling around the manger-cradle accords well with the other elements of this Gospel which make it one of great human appeal.

I. Who Were the Shepherds?

It seems especially fitting that the birth of One Who was to be the Shepherd of His people should be announced to shepherds. And it was all the more appropriate that the announcement should be made in such a place. In the fields about Bethlehem there yet remained fragrant memories of Ruth and Boaz, of Jesse and David. David spent his youth in those pastures about Bethlehem tending his father's flocks. There he fought the lion and the bear and slew them. There he received the inspiration to write the gentle, trustful words of the Shepherd Psalm: "The Lord is my shepherd, I shall not want." There, according to the prophet Micah, the hopes of Israel were to be fulfilled by the coming of the Messiah:

> "And thou Bethlehem, land of Judah,
> Art in no wise least among the princes of Judah:
> For out of thee shall come forth a governor,
> Who shall be shepherd of my people Israel."

The years hastened on by prophet-bards foretold and on a certain never-to-be forgotten night, while the shepherds were abiding in the fields keeping watch over their flocks they were suddenly startled out of their drowsy vigil by the appearance of an angel of the Lord who announced to them the good tidings of the birth of the Saviour. The angel also described to the shepherds the sign by which they were to verify the truth of the proclamation, that is, they were to find a babe wrapped in swaddling clothes, and lying in a manger. This pronouncement was followed by the sudden appearance of a multitude of the heavenly host praising God, and saying:

"Glory to God in the highest,
And on earth peace among men in whom he is well pleased."

Who were these shepherds whom God so highly honored by sending to them His messenger with the tidings of the birth of His Son? We cannot learn a great deal more about them than is given in the Gospel record. Story tellers of reverent imagination have dealt with the theme of the shepherds, and have endeavored to make them more real to us. Henry van Dyke in his beautiful story, "Even Unto Bethlehem", names four of the shepherds as follows: Zadok, Jotham, Shama, and Nathan. He also indicates that there was a fifth shepherd whose story is told in his tale of "The Sad Shepherd."

Jewish history adds somewhat to our knowledge of these shepherds and brings to our attention certain facts that are less familiar than the Gospel story. It was a well established conviction among the Jews that the Messiah was to be born at Bethlehem. The belief that the Messiah was to be revealed from Migdal Eder, "the tower of the flock", was equally well settled. This Migdal Eder, or tower of the flock, was a watch-tower for the flocks that pastured close to the town of Bethlehem on the road to Jerusalem. The flocks pastured in this vicinity were destined for Temple-sacrifices, and accordingly the shepherds who watched over them were not ordinary shepherds. The Rabbis had imposed a ban upon ordinary shepherds on account of their isolated manner of life which rendered strict observance of religious ordinances unlikely, if not impossible. But the shepherds who kept the flocks for the Temple-sacrifices belonged to a different class. They were acceptable to the Rabbis because they could come to the Temple for the legal observances. Another distinguishing factor was that the Temple-

flocks lay out in the fields all the year round, and were not shel-
tered in the sheep-folds during the winter weather. The shepherds,
therefore, watched these flocks all the year round, taking their turns
by day and by night. Thus we see that in some dim manner Jewish tradition had foreseen that the first revelation of the Messiah
would come from that Migdal Eder where shepherds watched their
flocks all the year round. Is this not a suggestion of the constant
vigilance and expectation that are always necessary on the part of
those who would receive new experiences of His coming into their
lives?

The other details of the story are as familiar to us as the words of
an old song. Let us then give heed to some of the abiding truths
that come as angel voices calling us to rise up and seek the Saviour.

II. Why Were the Shepherds Afraid?

Let us consider the message the shepherds heard on that wonderful night. The initial words of the herald-angel were: "Be not
afraid." But the shepherds were afraid; they were sore afraid.
They were startled and terrified by the heavenly glory that fell in
a flood upon them, and by the appearance of the shining one who
addressed them in words they could understand. Why were the
shepherds afraid? Ah, that is the truth we need to know, for it reveals to us how mankind sorely needed the Saviour God sent into
the world! Why were they afraid? Not because they had done any
wrong; not because their consciences troubled them; not because
they feared physical harm. They were afraid because they were
utterly unaccustomed to such intimate contact with heavenly beings.
Good men that they were, they still realized their unworthiness to
be found in the presence of Deity. We have proceeded into Luke's
Gospel only to the tenth verse of the second chapter and three times
these words have occurred: "Be not afraid." In chapter one, verse
thirteen, the record is that the angel who appeared to Zacharias
said, "Fear not, Zacharias." And in verse thirty, it is recorded that
the angel who appeared to Mary said, "Fear not, Mary." These
pious Israelites experienced the same fear that Peter, James, and
John felt on the Holy Mount when they heard the voice out of
heaven saying, "This is my beloved Son, in whom I am well
pleased; hear ye him." It was the same fear the disciples felt when
they were in the storm-tossed boat on the lake and Jesus came to

them, walking on the sea. It was the same fear that shook Peter's soul after Jesus' miracle of the draught of fishes when he cried out, "Depart from me; for I am a sinful man, O Lord." It was the same fear the women felt when they were hastening from the empty tomb on Easter morning, and Jesus appeared to them in the way and directed them to tell His disciples to meet Him in Galilee.

These instances of fearfulness in the presence of deity teach us a solemn truth. They tell us plainly that man has fallen from his original estate; that men are not on as good terms with Heaven as they ought to be; that even the best and purest of earth are estranged from the holiness of Heaven. The flaming sword has never been removed from the Garden of Eden where man first lived in perfect fellowship with his Maker.

DeWolf Hopper, in his autobiography, "Once a Clown, Always a Clown," describes the play, "The Model," by Byron Ongley as follows: "The action took place in the Paris studio of a young English artist. . . . The artist is painting a Biblical scene, and unable to find among professional models a face that suggests the spiritual demands of the Christ, he sends his servant out to scour the streets. The servant is long on the quest, but returns at last with a splendid young peasant with a natural blonde beard. The artist instructs the servant to show the peasant into another room and make him up for the subject. Meanwhile a half-drunken crowd of fellow artists, students and models have gathered in the studio. The party verges on an orgy and an old libertine, approaching senility, shakes his head at the scene. He offers himself as a horrible example of a misspent life, but Youth flouts his moralizing.

"In the midst of the orgy the model, garbed for his role, appears without warning on the platform. A woman sees him first and faints without a sound. Another woman espies him, her wine glass shatters on the floor and she screams hysterically. An awesome hush follows, every eye turned toward the figure on the platform, and the old roue, standing aghast for a moment, drops to the floor, dead."

"In the midst of you standeth one whom ye know not." Oh, how He rebukes the iniquity, the sin and the wickedness of this evil world! Oh, what a revelation He brings of the distance between the sinfulness of man and the holiness of God! Oh, what a plea He makes for the wicked to forsake their way and to return unto the Lord that He may have mercy upon them and abundantly pardon! "For God so loved the world, that he gave his only begotten Son, that whosoever believeth on him should not perish, but have eternal life. For God sent not the Son into the world to judge the world; but that the world should be saved through him." "Behold, the Lamb of God, that taketh away the sin of the world!" God sent His Son into the world to remove this barrier of unholy fear; to reconcile lost sinners of earth with the holy God of heaven. He sent His Son in the likeness of human flesh that we might behold the glory of the Father in heaven, and at the same time learn of His compassion and love for us and accept the way He has opened to us to return to the Paradise we had lost.

III. What Did the Shepherds Hear?

After seeking to calm the fears of the trembling shepherds, the angel-herald spoke to them the wonderful words: "Behold, I bring you good tidings of great joy which shall be to all the people: for there is born to you this day in the city of David a Saviour, who is Christ the Lord." The glad tidings of great joy which thrilled the hearts of the wondering shepherds heralded the momentous event of the Saviour's birth; the coming into the world of the long-expected Messiah. And this good news was for all people because He came to be the Saviour of the world.

The world into which the Christ-Child was born needed above all else a Saviour, One Who could save His people from their sins. It was a dark, cruel, helpless and hopeless world into which Jesus was born. It is very difficult for us in this far-off day to realize what a needy age it was . The greatest need of that age was for a Saviour. Its primary need was not for a king; not for a mighty warrior; not for a wise law-giver; not for a great philosopher; not for a prophet, but for a Saviour. The ancient world supremely needed One Who could bind up the bruised and broken hearts of a degraded and oppressed people; One Who could take the whole terrible burden of the world's guilt and sin upon Himself and give deliverance and peace to a captive race.

And lo, such a Saviour had come! This Saviour was to be not only the Shepherd of His people Israel, but the Saviour Who was to take away the sins of the whole world. There is special significance in the fact that the announcement of the Saviour's birth came to shepherds; to men who under ordinary conditions belonged to a class held in contempt by the religious rulers of the time. For this Saviour was to be the Saviour of all the people. These shepherds were received by Him Who called Himself the Good Shepherd. The despised publicans and outcasts, Matthew, Zachaeus, and others, were among the lost sheep to be gathered in. Poor, besmirched sinners like the woman of Samaria were to have their guilty stains washed away. Proud Pharisees like Saul of Tarsus were to find the peace which comes only through faith in Jesus Christ. God-fearing Gentiles such as Cornelius and Lydia were to find in Him the true light for which they had been seeking. And all pious Israelites like Simeon and Anna, like Mary of Bethany and a host of others,, were to realize their fondest hopes and dreams in the coming of Him who was the Consolation of Israel.

The world in our day is no different from the world into which Jesus came with respect to its greatest need. The supreme need of the modern world is still for a Saviour, for the Saviour, Jesus Christ the Son of God. Multitudes of men and women need Him to save them from their sins, and to be a Companion and Helper amid the perplexities, trials, burdens, and sorrows of their lives. The lost generation of youth need to find in Him the Bright and Morning Star so that He can shine in upon their hearts and give them purity, peace and hope. The nations of the world torn and bleeding with hatred, war, and fratricidal strife; reeking with greed, injustice and oppression; rotting with the appalling cancer of crime and the ruinous deluge of debauchery; dismayed and distressed by the tidal wave of apostacy, godlessness and unbelief— the nations of the world need as never before the salvation of God in Jesus Christ. They need the healing, saving, restoring love of God the Father; His forgiving mercy, grace and compassion; His Spirit of righteousness, peace and joy; His Kingdom of love, good will and world-wide brotherhood. Life abundant, for men and nations; peace that passes understanding, for men and nations; salvation, full, free and permanent, for men and nations God graciously offers in the Gospel of His Son, the Good Shepherd of all the sheep. May God grant that at Christmas time and throughout the years to be the good tidings of great joy may be heard with saving power by many peoples the world around.

WHAT THE SHEPHERDS FOUND

Patient Shepherds

Patient shepherds keeping
 Watches of the night;
Drowsy shepherds, sleeping,
 Wakened by a light
Flashing, flowing, leaping—
 Shepherds, what a sight!

Shepherds clothed in glory
 From the flaming sky,
Angels singing, "Glory"
 Heaven drawing nigh;
Heaven singing, "Glory"—
 Shepherds wonder why.

Angels homeward flying,
 Shepherds on the lea
Asking and replying,
 "How can such things be?"
Heaven's lights all dying—
 "Let us go and see!"

Shepherds, did you find Him?
 Did the angel say,
"They that seek shall find Him
 Every Christmas day?"
Where to go to find Him—
 Did the angel say?
—REV. LOUIS F. BENSON, 1927.

(Used by permission)

VIII

What the Shepherds Found

Luke 2:16, *And they came with haste, and found both Mary and Joseph, and the babe lying in the manger.*

MATTHEW'S Gospel is the Gospel of the King and it is fitting that he should tell that portion of the story of the birth of Jesus which brings into prominence the kingly qualities of the Saviour. Hence Matthew relates the story of the visit of the Wise-men from the East who came with royal retinue and offered princely gifts to the Christ-Child in acknowledgment of Him as their new-born King. The Gospel of Luke is the Gospel of the Ideal Man, the Gospel of Humanity. It is likewise fitting that Luke should narrate the story of the visit of the shepherds which emphasizes the humble, lowly, human aspects of the birth of Jesus. The Gospel of Luke has been called "the most beautiful book in the world," and surely there is no more beautiful chapter in this book than that which tells of the birth of the Ideal Man and the adoration of the humble shepherds.

I. The Shepherds' Faith.

St. Luke tells us how the shepherds received the message of the angels. After the last strains of the hymn of glory and of peace had died away and the angelic host had disappeared into heaven, the bewildered shepherds fell to talking to one another about the miraculous event. They kept repeating to one another, "Let us go now even unto Bethlehem, and see this thing that is come to pass, which the Lord has made known to us."

Observe that the shepherds straightway believed the proclamation of the angels. There was no trace of doubt in their minds that these things were so. There was no time wasted in idle speculation as to the 'how' or 'why' or 'wherefore' of what had occurred. They did not seek to account for the appearance of the angels or

77

the message of the herald or the hymn of the angelic choir by saying that it had been a dream or a vision or an hallucination. They accepted the evidence that had been presented to their senses and they believed that the whole supernatural event had been made known to them by the Lord. So sure were they of the truth of the angel's message that they said one to another: "Let us now go . . . and see this thing that is come to pass." They were absolutely confident that when they arrived in the village of Bethlehem they would find the babe wrapped in swaddling clothes, and lying in a manger.

Thank God that, in a dark and unbelieving age, there were humble, faithful, simple-hearted shepherds to receive the message of the angels! In our day there are blind and bitter agnostics like Clarence Darrow who tell us that these miraculous events could not have happened; that they did not happen. In like manner the rationalists, who are more sophisticated than reasonable, are saying about the same thing. They explain away every supernatural event recorded in the Bible and substitute some absurd hypothesis conceived by their own foolish logic which requires a vast deal more of faith to believe than the simple facts as they are recorded in the Gospels! One such rationalist, (his name is not important in this connection) has recently stated in a profound book on theology that the miracles are instances of the "kindergarten methods" which God employed in the childhood of the race. I suppose we are to infer from this that Moses, Elijah, Jesus and Paul belonged to the childhood of the race, and that these modern naturalistic perverters of the truth belong to the full-grown manhood of the race! Thank God for the childlike faith that receives the declarations of the Gospel as true! Do these rationalists not yet know the essential truth of the Gospel that they must become as little children before they can enter the kingdom of heaven? These sophisticated moderns, who are not as modern as they think themselves to be, try to tell us what really did happen when Jesus was born as though they were there, as though they had seen with their own eyes! Personally, I much prefer to have the shepherds, the fishermen, the tax-collectors and the physicians tell me what happened; I am entirely satisfied to have these divinely accredited witnesses tell me about the things they saw and heard and received into their hearts as they were moved to tell them by the Holy Spirit of God!

II. The Shepherds' Reward.

The shepherds not only believed the word of the angel, but they were very urgent in acting upon their belief. We do not know what disposition they made of their flocks of sheep, but at any rate they departed at once on their mission of verification. They had but to cross a comparatively short stretch of intervening country to reach the edge of the village, and once there they would experience no difficulty in finding the lantern above the doorway which led to the manger within. The record is that "they came with haste, and found both Mary and Joseph, and the babe lying in the manger."

Those who would find the Christ-Child must not delay. They must act upon every impulse and every message that directs them to the manger scene. They must forsake every occupation; they must break every tie that hinders them from going on the sacred quest. "The king's business requireth haste." Those who delay for a moment may find that it is too late. Those who fail to heed the counsels of the messengers of God prompting them to seek the lowly Christ will be denied the rapture of His beatific smile. We must go not only once, but we must return again and again. For only as our hearts are continuously filled with the truths and influences that center in the cradle of Bethlehem will the music of the angels and the spirit of good will and peace be kept alive in the world.

III. The Shepherds' Witness.

In this old-new story we read that the shepherds published their knowledge abroad. Not merely to Joseph and Mary did they relate the wonderful saying of the angel concerning this Child, but also to the inhabitants of Bethlehem generally. They told everybody they met about the glad tidings of great joy for all people. They told the other shepherds who relieved them in keeping the Temple flocks; they told the priests and the worshipers they met when they went up to the Temple; they told their families and friends, and all the honest people about Bethlehem and vicinity. And all that heard it wondered at the things which were spoken unto them by the shepherds. But Mary, the happy mother, kept all these sayings, pondering them in her heart. The shepherds returned to the care of their sheep, glorifying and praising God for all the things that they had heard and seen, even as it was spoken unto them. And all who heard their story glorified and praised God. So it came to pass at that first Christmas that all humble and believing hearts who heard the story found a deeper joy and peace than they had ever known before.

Upon all who have heard the good news of the Christmas message there rests the responsibility of publishing that good news abroad. It is a hard way to Bethlehem — it was a hard way for Joseph and Mary and a hard way for the Wise-men — and there are many people in the world who have not yet found the Saviour. Perhaps there are those who will not find the way unless we make it plain to them. Perhaps there are those who will not be able to hear the music of the angels in this world of sin and woe unless we help them to hear. Perhaps there are some who will not know the peace and joy and hope that are a part of the Christmas spirit unless they catch these notes from our lives. There are some who may never hear the story of God's love for them, as they are entitled to hear it, unless they hear it from our lips. How many have kept their hearts pure and tender and gentle for the telling of the sweetest story ever told, the story of God's love expressed in the unspeakable gift of His only begotten Son Whom the adoring shepherds found as a little babe wrapped in swaddling clothes, and lying in a manger? How many fathers and mothers are wise enough faithfully to tell the story of the birth of Jesus to their children so that they will always understand the real significance of Christmas and will always love the Saviour better with each coming of the holy time?

I had a dear friend at home, an old lady who was very kind and good to me a number of years ago. As she advanced in years she suddenly became totally blind for no reason that the doctors could give. She was compelled to spend her later years in a very helpless and lonely state. In earlier years she had sacrificed much and invested much in the care of a niece whom she reared from childhood. In due time this niece was married and moved into her own home. She took with her the radio her aunt had given her as a present some time before. She took the radio with her and left her old aunt to her darkness and loneliness, uncheered by the consolation of radio music and companionship! When I heard the story I thought it one of the worst examples of selfishness and ingratitude of which I had ever heard. "Is there any cause in nature that makes these hard hearts?"

As we think about it, the popular manner of celebrating Christmas is equally deserving of blame. People sitting in darkness and in the land of the shadow of death are deprived of the consolation of heaven-born music by reason of the selfishness, preoccupation and neglect of those who ought to be living witnesses and loving ambassadors of Christ's salvation for mankind. We may be sure that the lowly Christ, the ministering Servant, places higher value upon the kindnesses we render to the poor and needy, the sick and lonely, the sorrowful and discouraged than He does upon the vast amount of wealth expended to make sumptuous feasts and luxurious holidays for those whose lives are already surfeited with pleasures and over-supplied with material things. The real Christmas challenge the faithful shepherds hold before all lovers of the Lord of Glory is this:

"Go and tell unto all the gospel story,
    They wait for the light of His word;
They wait for the Messenger of glory,
    Of whom they as yet have not heard.

O who will tell the story old,
The story of redemption ever new?
O who will bring them to the fold?
The Lord is waiting for you."

THREE GLIMPSES OF THE CHRIST CHILD

Jesus, Child of Bethlehem!

Jesus, Child of Bethlehem,
Bringing neither gold nor gem;
Crowned with love's bright diadem.
    Hallelujah!

Mary watching by His bed,
In the lowly cattle shed;
Mindful of what angels said.
    Hallelujah!

Angels on the wings of light
Singing carols in the night,
Making earth like heaven bright.
    Hallelujah!

Shepherds listening, as they sing
Glory to the newborn King;
To the Christ their homage bring.
    Hallelujah!

Wise men following from afar,
Guided by the wondrous star,
Where the Child and mother are.
    Hallelujah!

Gold they gave as to a King,
Incense as to God they bring,
Myrrh that speaks of suffering.
    Hallelujah!

Glory in the highest sing,
Peace on earth He comes to bring,
Praise we now our God and King.
    Hallelujah!

—Rev. Hugh Thomson Kerr, 1925.
(Used by permission of the author)

IX

12/24{27/1959

Three Glimpses of the Christ Child

LUKE 2:16, *And they came with haste, and found both Mary and Joseph, and the babe lying in the manger.*

LUKE 2:27-28, *And he came in the Spirit into the temple: and when the parents brought in the child Jesus, that they might do concerning him after the custom of the law, then he received him into his arms, and blessed God, . . .*

MATTHEW 2:11, *And they came into the house and saw the young child with Mary his mother; and they fell down and worshipped him; and opening their treasures they offered unto him gifts, gold and frankincense and myrrh.*

THE Christmas story gives us three glimpses of the Christ Child which we wish to consider in this message. Perhaps it has never clearly dawned upon the consciousness of some that we have only three brief glimpses of the Christ Child. The world seems so filled with Christmas and our hearts so completely satisfied with the sacred story that we may pause to wonder how these few scenes could cast such a holy spell upon the world. These scenes of His birth are indeed like the tiny grain of mustard seed, "which indeed is less than all seeds; but when it is grown. it is greater than the herbs, and becometh a tree, so that the birds of the heaven come and lodge in the branches thereof."

We should like to give a clear description of each of these three separate scenes. We should like to have you see each scene distinctly by itself and learn the meaning of each. Why is this important? Because in the minds of many people there are confused if not conglomerated ideas of the Nativity scenes. It is really amazing that this should be so, but it shows how careless and inaccurate we are about rightly interpreting the Word of truth. For example, I once heard a Sunday School teacher telling her children the Christmas story. She was telling about the shepherds and she said something like this. "The shepherds were keeping watch over their sheep, when an angel appeared to them and told them about the birth of the Saviour in Bethlehem. When the angels went away into heaven, the shepherds saw a bright star in the sky and they followed this star till it brought them to the manger where they found Mary and Joseph, and the babe lying in the manger." I have always felt that the Christmas story was wonderful enough without adding to its miraculous character! As a matter of fact, nothing at all is said about a star in connection with the visit of the shepherds. Neither did the Wise-men see a vision of angels. The shepherds and the Wise-men did not visit the holy family at the same time, as some of the great paintings of the Nativity indicate. For the sake of accuracy and a better understanding of the meaning of Christmas it is important that we should consider each separate scene by itself. Let us then examine more closely these three glimpses of the infant Saviour.

I. In the Stable — The Shepherds.

The first glimpse we have of the new-born Saviour is in the stable at Bethlehem. Let us approach this scene the way Joseph and Mary approached it. Joseph and Mary were dwelling in Nazareth when they first received heaven's message of the Saviour's coming birth. The journey from Nazareth to Bethlehem was made during the few days prior to Holy Night. Have we ever thought of what this journey would mean? Mary's foreboding on the eve of the journey is thus imagined by Henry van Dyke in his story, "Even Unto Bethlehem". "Oh, Joseph, do you see what that means for us? We must go to Bethlehem, the city of the family of David. I am terribly afraid of that long, hard journey now, with my time so near. What if we should run into some danger? What if an accident should befall me? What if I should lose the child I carry, the hope of Israel? I could not bear it. Ah, woe is me! Woe is me!" But Caesar Augustus had spoken, and the journey must be made. The distance was a hundred miles. But they could not cover the distance in a few hours over broad highways in a smooth-riding automobile. They could not enjoy the safety and comfort of a stream-lined railroad coach. No, the journey must be made in part on donkey-back and a great part of the way on foot. The route they followed descended from the hills of Nazareth to the

Jordan Valley, traversed the east bank of the Jordan River to Jericho, and ascended the hills of Judaea to Bethlehem. The story teller writes: "There were no angelic wings to bear them up and carry them over the rough places, lest Mary should bruise her foot against a stone. No rich traveller rolling by offered them a lift in his chariot; they were too humble and poor for that courtesy. Nor was there any miracle to remove the hardships or shorten the weary miles of the long, long way. It was plain plodding. Step after step they must measure the hundred miles, with only poor little Thistles to carry the scanty luggage and to let Mary ride on his back now and then, when she was too tired to put one foot before the other."

After five weary days of travelling they came towards nightfall "over the last rugged hill into the little town of Bethlehem." Mary was not received into a hospital room with clean, white beds. She was not cared for by a corps of nurses trained to do everything that needed to be done for the patient's well being. No efficient doctor, a little sleepy and grumpy perhaps, but efficient nonetheless, was at hand to render expert care. This was ancient Judaea, the obscure town of Bethlehem, and no one expected the anguished couple. The town was filled to overflowing with the many visitors who had come to enrol on the tax lists. There was no possibility of finding room in the inn. So they found refuge in a stable in the inn-yard, and there Mary brought forth her promised Son, and wrapped him in swaddling clothes, and laid him in a manger.

The stable was not like any we have ever seen in this country, but it was just an ordinary stable of Bethlehem. It was not built of wood, but it was a dry grotto or cave dug out of the face of the cliff. In it there were stalls for oxen and other beasts of burden, with their customary bedding of straw and their mangers for holding rough feed. Let us not be bedazzled by poetic fancy or artistic imagination. This was not the kind of a stable painted by some of the great artists. It did not look more like a castle than a stable! It was just a plain, rude, ordinary stable. It looked like a stable and it smelled like a stable. This odor might be regarded as unpleasant by some, but not by those who are accustomed to working around stables. The roof was low, the place was dimly lighted, the ceiling was festooned with cobwebs, the walls were smoky and dirty. The oxen and the donkeys were in their stalls, not a little disquieted by the strange sounds and motions in the neighboring stall. But before long all became calm and peaceful. The new-born baby was fast asleep in his clean bed of straw. It was not a bright, freshly painted dainty little bed arranged with sweet baby pillows and covers, but the baby Jesus did not know the difference. No strange hands had handled him either, for the mother with her own pale hands had wrapped his little body with long white bands of linen which she had prepared for the hour of need. They were all exhausted from the ordeal and mother, baby and faithful Joseph slept the sleep of the just.

Not long after, there came a gentle knocking on the rude door of the stable and a group of men whose faces were bronzed with sun and wind and lighted with wonder and reverence came in to kneel and worship at what they found. The babe was just a few hours old and the light of heaven was unmistakably clear on his little face. His eyes were still fast shut in slumber. There was no halo around his tiny head; he was just a plump, healthy, beautiful baby boy. The shepherds told Mary and Joseph the wonderful tidings they had received from the angels concerning this child, and they and other kindly visitors who came to the stable wondered at the sayings of the shepherds. But Mary's heart was filled with rapture and a great peace. The gentle shepherds closed the stable door behind them, and went out into the clear morning to face a new world filled with gladness and hope.

Is it needful to point any moral? The manger scene is of one piece with the humility that characterized the Saviour's entire life upon earth. The Lord of Glory humbled Himself: He was cradled in a rude manger; He was reared in a humble home; He plied a humble trade; He ministered as a lowly Servant; He humbled Himself, becoming obedient even unto death, yea, the death of the cross. As we meditate upon the meaning of this glimpse of the infant Saviour, we may be sure that the lesson He would have all of His disciples learn by heart is this: "Come unto me, all ye that labor and are heavy laden, . . . Take my yoke upon you, and learn of me; for I am meek and lowly in heart; and ye shall find rest unto your souls."

II. In the Temple — The Saints.

The second glimpse we have of the Christ Child is in the Temple. We are now in Jerusalem. The child Jesus is forty days old. The parents have journeyed from Bethlehem to Jerusalem, a short distance of five miles. This was an easy and happy journey. They brought their firstborn Son up to the Temple that they might do concerning him after the custom of the law. The law of Moses required that a firstborn son be presented to the Lord and dedicated to His service. The law also required that a sacrifice for a sin-offering be made for the purification of the mother. The sacrifice of a lamb was required of those who could afford it, but the sacrifice of a pair of young pigeons was acceptable from the poor. The parents made this humble offering and the priest declared the ransom price of the firstborn paid.

This simple rite, practiced by the faithful for many generations, was now to be invested with new meaning. There was in the Temple a venerable saint by the name of Simeon to whom it had been revealed by the Holy Spirit that he should not see death, before he had seen the Lord's Christ. This aged man now received the six-weeks old baby Jesus into his frail arms and blessed God, saying:

> "Now lettest thou thy servant depart, Lord,
> According to thy word, in peace;
> For mine eyes have seen thy salvation,
> Which thou hast prepared before the face of all peoples;
> A light for revelation to the Gentiles,
> And the glory of thy people Israel."

A pious old praying woman by the name of Anna likewise acclaimed Mary's child as the Messiah and published abroad her joyous faith to all them that were looking for the redemption of Jerusalem.

In this scene the Christmas message is for ever linked with the Temple of God. "Whom God hath joined together, let no man put asunder!" The example of the parents' obedience to the commands of God as centered in the Temple worship is an example for the godly in all ages to follow. Surely the Christmas message cannot be kept alive in the world apart from the Church-centered worship of God in Christ by the people. Christmas observances divorced from spiritual worship in the House of God cannot long perpetuate the singular beauty and dynamic of Christmas.

In this Temple scene we are shown again the kind of people who receive the Christ. They are those whose hearts are prepared to receive Him. They are those who love God, who hope in His Word, who are faithful to His commandments. They are those who are ever seeking first the Kingdom of God and His righteousness; who are ever longing for the redemption and consolation of the people of God; who are ever devoting their prayers, energies, possessions and lives to this end.

III. In the Home — The Wise-Men.

The third glimpse we have of the Christ Child is in the home. The scene includes the mother and Child and the Wise-men. "And they came into the house and saw the young child with Mary his mother; and they fell down and worshipped him; and opening their treasures they offered unto him gifts, gold and frankincense and myrrh." We know this home was in Bethlehem, but we do not know whose home it was. In all probability it was the home of friends of Joseph and Mary in Bethlehem. We know this scene took place after the presentation of the Child in the Temple, and before the flight into Egypt and return to Nazareth. But we cannot know exactly how old Jesus was when the Wise-men saw Him. We are told in the record that Herod learned from the Wise-men exactly what time the star appeared to them in the east. With this knowledge in mind, Herod accordingly issued his cruel decree to slaughter all the male children that were in Bethlehem, from two years old and under. From this we infer that Jesus was about two years old when the Wise-men saw Him, that is, if He was born when the star first appeared to the Wise-men in the east. Joseph was living at the time, but his name is not mentioned in connection with the visit of the Wise-men. While these princely visitors were in the house, was not the faithful Joseph keeping watch to see that no hostile enemy approached the place? He must have feared something of the kind, for immediately after the Wise-men had departed Joseph was warned by an angel of the Lord in a dream to take the young child and his mother, and flee into Egypt.

The worship of the Wise-men and their presentation of precious gifts to the Christ Child suggest the abiding truths that Christ is worthy to be worshipped as God, and that He is supremely entitled to the best gifts of life, service, and substance that men can give to Him. As representatives of the Gentile world they are the first fruits of that unnumbered throng of many brethren of all lands and peoples that should receive Christ as Saviour and own Him as Lord and King.

That this worship was centered in a home—in an unknown and unnamed home—teaches us a great lesson concerning the place Christmas should occupy in all Christian homes. Happily, Christmas is very largely a home-centered celebration. It is one of the brightest days in the whole year for the whole family, especially for little children. We owe all that is best in the home-life to the loving Saviour Who ever exalts and ennobles the family relationships and the home sanctities where He is known and honored. Speaking of Martin Luther, W. T. Hanzsche says, "Out of his beautiful home life came 'Away in a Manger, No Crib for a Bed,' one of our loveliest Christmas lullabies." We are grateful for the contributions all good homes make to the peace and happiness of the world. We are supremely grateful for the beautiful home life which nurtured the soul of Jesus and gave Him happy memories of His boyhood days during His later homeless years. We should all seek for His sake to foster the kind of home pictured for us in this closing scene of the Christmas story; the home where Jesus is welcomed, worshipped, and served with the best gifts of love His people can lay at His feet.

HOW GOD SPOKE TO THE WISE-MEN

As With Gladness Men of Old

As with gladness men of old
Did the guiding star behold;
As with joy they hailed its light,
Leading onward, beaming bright;
So, most gracious God, may we
Evermore be led to Thee.

As with joyful steps they sped
To that lowly manger-bed,
There to bend the knee before
Him whom heaven and earth adore;
So may we with willing feet
Ever seek Thy mercy-seat.

As they offered gifts most rare
At that manger rude and bare; ;
So may we with holy joy,
Pure, and free from sin's alloy,
All our costliest treasures bring,
Christ, to Thee, our heavenly King.

Holy Jesus, every day
Keep us in the narrow way;
And, when earthly things are past,
Bring our ransomed souls at last
Where they need no star to guide,
Where no clouds Thy glory hide.

In the heavenly country bright
Need they no created light;
Thou its Light, its Joy, its Crown,
Thou its Sun which goes not down;
There for ever may we sing
Alleluias to our King.

—William C. Dix, 1861.

X

How God Spoke to the Wise-Men

MATTHEW 2:19, *And they, having heard the king, went their way; and lo, the star, which they saw in the east, went before them, till it came and stood over where the young child was.*

CHRISTMAS stands supremely for the blending of the earthly and the heavenly. It is the better Jacob's Ladder let down from above to connect man's earth with God's heaven. Christmas opens the windows of heaven and gives us glimpses of the invisible and eternal world. A strange new star shines in the sky. Angelic hosts sing from the portals of heaven. Men and women see glorious visions and dream beautiful dreams. The Book gives forth its marvelous secrets. A Child is given by miraculous birth. The spirit of prophecy breaks forth. Rulers are troubled and kingdoms are shaken. All things come to pass according to ancient oracles. Events move in mysterious sequence to a harmonious conclusion, as though marshalled by an over-ruling Hand, as indeed they are.

The wisdom of Christmas lies in accepting all these things as true, and in yielding ourselves to these spiritual forces that lie about us. We will be the 'Wise-men' of our clime and country if we do this. God spoke to the Wise-men of the east through various mediums, and He continues to reveal His mysteries to those who are wise enough to seek His Divine guidance and help. Matthew's story of the visit of the Wise-men reveals four ways in which God made Himself known to them.

I. God Spoke to the Wise-Men Through the Star.

First of all, God spoke to the Wise-men through the star. The pre-eminently remarkable thing about their coming to Jerusalem is that they were guided by the star which they saw in the east. These

95

princely travellers were probably Persian Magi who were versed
in the study of the stars and who were familiar with certain prophecies of the Old Testament Scriptures. We can imagine them por-
ing over their mystic scroll and reading the words of Balaam's
prophecy:

> "I see him, but not now;
> I behold him, but not nigh:
> There shall come forth a star out of Jacob,
> And a sceptre shall rise out of Israel."

In the fulness of time the "star out of Jacob" appeared and they regarded it as the heavenly sign of the Messiah's birth. They came
to Jerusalem seeking information concerning the new-born "King
of the Jews" and were directed to Bethlehem. Once more the star
which they saw in the east appeared and guided them to the very
house where the Christ-child was.

The stars have always spoken to upreaching minds the thoughts
of the eternal God. They have always helped to guide questing
souls to their journey's end. They have always served as guiding
beacon's in the darkness of night. The travellers of the East from
time immemorial guided their caravans across the desert sands by
the aid of the stars. Navigators on the seven seas of the world have
charted their courses by the starry map of the skies. And now the
pilots of the air take their bearings from these eternal sky-marks.
In the month of November, 1935, the "China Clipper" on its epoch-
al flight across the Pacific from California to Manila demonstrated
this. While out over the Pacific with no view even of the ocean,
the Navigation Officer gave this report by radio: "I clambored
through the aft hatch to secure our bearings from the skies and to
glimpse old Polaris with his other starry guideposts. . . . We of the
China Clipper can plot our program westward by the focal points
in the sky. In other words, if we had to, we could rely on celestial
navigation." It is a long, long stretch from the camel trains of the
eastern deserts to the gigantic airliners of the Pacific—but the
starry guideposts are still standing!

The stars have also spoken their messages of spiritual guidance,
wisdom and consolation to men of all ages. Poets have ever been
inspired by the glories of the starry heavens. One of the greatest
poetical tributes to the stars in literature is that of Dante who con-

cludes each of the three sections of his "Divine Comedy" with the word 'stars'. This literary artifice is ample evidence of what the stars meant to the great Italian poet. The Hebrew poet fixed his gaze upon the wonders of the Syrian night and cried:

> "When I consider thy heavens, the work of thy fingers,
> The moon and the stars, which thou hast ordained;
> What is man, that thou art mindful of him?
> And the son of man, that thou visitest him?"

Even so God will speak many things to our souls—the things of peace, trust and tranquillity—if we lift our eyes to the light of the stars.

II. God Spoke to the Wise--Men Through the Book.

Again, God spoke to the Wise-men through the Book. We have already observed that they were undoubtedly familiar with the Old Testament prophecies. It was their contact with the Scriptures that first implanted in their souls the hope of the promised Messiah, the bright and morning Star. Then when they came to Jerusalem on their important quest, it was the light of the Word that sent them on to Bethlehem. For the chief priests and scribes, turning to the prophecy of Micah, read to king Herod concerning the birthplace of Messiah:

> "And thou Bethlehem, land of Judah,
> Art in no wise least among the princes of Judah:
> For out of thee shall come forth a governor,
> Who shall be shepherd of my people Israel."

The chief priests and scribes evidently had not taken this word to heart, but the Wise-men, continuing their star-lit journey, found it to be even as the prophet had spoken.

The Bible is the written record of God's Word to men. Through it God speaks to all those who have ears to hear. Through it He reveals His character, His will, His purposes to redeem humanity. Through it He reveals man's sin, man's need of redemption, man's immortal destiny as a redeemed child of God.

The Scriptures have been received into the hearts of uncounted myriads of people as the very Word of God. The hopes of the pious Israelites who were ready for Messiah's coming were founded upon the promises of God in their Scriptures. The Songs of Mary and Zacharias are veritable mosiacs of Old Testament passages. Jesus Himself received the Scriptures as the written Word of God. He knew them by heart. He nourished His soul upon God's Word as the very bread of life. He met and conquered all of the temptations of His life by relying upon the Word of God. He took one of the prophecies of Isaiah as the text of His life and as the program of His ministry. His last word upon the cross was a quotation from the Psalms. Christ never had any difficulty in hearing His Father speak to Him through the Book. From it He learned to render perfect obedience to the will of God. "Lo, I am come (in the roll of the book it is written of me) To do thy will, O God."

The Bible contains all necessary wisdom, guidance and counsel for the needs of the world to-day. The Bible way of life has not been very generally or very intensively tried. If we were really to search the Scriptures we would find in them eternal life. The Bible is quite generally known about, but comparatively few people have struck upon the untold hidden treasure it contains. If we long for spiritual power, for moral courage, for assurance concerning the life to be, we will get these things when we read our Bibles again. We will find the Book to be all that the Psalmist claims for it:

> "Thy word is a lamp unto my feet,
> And light unto my path."

The Bible is the only Book in the world that tells us of the earthly life of the Son of God. The Bible is the only Book that gives us Immanuel—God with us. It is the only Book that tells us how we may become children of God, by faith in the Son of God Who loved us and gave Himself up for us. When Sir Walter Scott lay dying, he said to his son-in-law, "Bring me the Book." "What book?" his son-in-law asked. "There is only one Book, the Bible," the dying man replied. "Bring me the Book." There is only one Book that reveals the way of eternal salvation in Jesus Christ the Son of God. This Book guided the Wise-men of the East to the

Christ-child, and it will guide every questing soul who earnestly seeks for the Light of Life to Him Who is the Shepherd and Bishop of our immortal souls.

III. God Spoke to the Wise-Men Through the Child.

Best of all, God spoke to the Wise-men through the Child. Their long journey across mountains, deserts and rivers was rewarded with the sight of Mary's child, who was the holy child begotten by the Spirit of God. "And they came into the house and saw the young child with Mary his mother; and they fell down and worshipped him; and opening their treasures they offered unto him gifts, gold and frankincense and myrrh."

The Nativity records contain some interesting and significant statements concerning this child. The angel Gabriel said to Mary concerning her son Jesus: "He shall be great, and shall be called the Son of the Most High: and the Lord God shall give unto him the throne of his father David: and he shall reign over the house of Jacob for ever; and of his kingdom there shall be no end. . . . wherefore also the holy thing which is begotten shall be called the Son of God." An angel of the Lord revealed the mystery to Joseph, saying, "And she shall bring forth a son; and thou shalt call his name JESUS; for it is he that shall save his people from their sins." The herald angel announced to the wondering shepherds: "Be not afraid; for behold, I bring you good tidings of great joy which shall be to all the people: for there is born to you this day in the city of David a Saviour, who is Christ the Lord." The venerable Simeon said to Mary the mother in the temple: "Behold, this child is set for the falling and the rising of many in Israel; and for a sign which is spoken against."

This is the Child the Wise-men saw and worshipped—the Christ-child, the son of David according to the flesh, the Son of God according to the Spirit. The hallowed glimpses we have of the holy Child in the stable, in the temple, and in the home all assure us that He is the well beloved and only begotten Son of God. He was probably about two years old when the Wise-men saw him in the house: a beautiful, normal, healthy, bright-eyed little boy. How His eyes would sparkle as the Wise-men offered their wonderful gifts to

Him! In His sweet little way He would smile upon these good men and thank them for their lovely gifts. The good men would never forget the smile that lighted up His beautiful face; that lighted up a whole new world for them.

God's crowning revelation of Himself to humanity came in the Person of His Son, Who came into the world as we came into the world and as our children come into the world. God has spoken to His people in many ways, but at last He spoke in and through His Son. The great message of Christmas is that "the Word became flesh, and dwelt among us" that we might behold the glory of "the only begotten from the Father, full of grace and truth." So it is that down through the years, the Christ-child first of all, and our own dear little children continue to lead us to the joy of Christmas and to the heart of the Father God.

IV. God Spoke to the Wise Men Through a Dream.

Lastly, God spoke to the Wise-men through a dream. They came, they found, they worshipped. Now they must return to their own country to spread the good news. The crafty king who trembled on his throne at Jerusalem had commanded the Wise-men to return to him with news of their Bethlehem discovery. But, "being warned of God in a dream that they should not return to Herod, they departed into their own country another way."

God has frequently revealed His will to His servants by means of dreams. He spoke to Jacob in a dream at Bethel; He spoke to Joseph in dreams and gave him the power to interpret dreams. Joseph, the husband of Mary, was prepared and sustained for his trying and heroic part in the Nativity drama by dreams sent from God. While our dreams are more often the result of over-burdened minds and over-worked stomachs, and are more often of the nightmare variety than of the heavenly vision type, yet it is nevertheless true that God does reveal His will through our subconscious natures in visions of the night. Our souls can be completely yielded up to God only when our subconscious as well as our conscious life is fully possessed and sanctified by the Holy Spirit of God. Let us believe that God can and does speak to His people in dreams and visions. Let us keep our hearts pure and be ready to obey the heavenly vision when God so chooses to speak to us. "And Joseph arose from his sleep, and did as the angel of the Lord commanded him."

We are all on a journey, a pilgrimage, a quest. We all need celestial guidance to take us over the mountains and through the valleys to the distant City that lies four-square. We need the Shepherd Star to bring us to Bethlehem—the House of Bread. The message of Christmas assures us that such guidance is available at all times to each one of us. God has spoken and continues to speak to us through His Word, His Son, His Spirit. If we follow His leading our feet will be kept on the high road that leads to the City of God.

PART THREE

WHAT CHRIST WANTS FOR CHRISTMAS

Angels, From the Realms of Glory

Angels, from the realms of glory,
  Wing your flight o'er all the earth;
Ye who sang creation's story,
  Now proclaim Messiah's birth:
    Come and worship,
    Come and worship,
  Worship Christ, the new-born King!

Shepherds, in the fields abiding,
  Watching o'er your flocks by night,
God with man is now residing,
  Yonder shines the infant Light:
    Come and worship,
    Come and worship,
  Worship Christ, the new-born King!

Sages, leave your contemplations,
  Brighter visions beam afar;
Seek the great Desire of nations;
  Ye have seen His natal star:
    Come and worship,
    Come and worship,
  Worship Christ, the new-born King!

Saints, before the altar bending,
  Watching long in hope and fear,
Suddenly the Lord, descending,
  In His temple shall appear:
    Come and worship,
    Come and worship,
  Worship Christ, the new-born King!

All creation, join in praising
  God the Father, Spirit, Son;
Evermore your voices raising
  To the Eternal Three in One:
    Come and worship,
    Come and worship,
  Worship Christ, the new-born King!
    —JAMES MONTGOMERY, 1816, 1825.

XI

What Christ Wants For Christmas

LUKE 2:17, *And when they saw it, they made known concerning the child with Mary his mother; and they fell down and worshipped him; and opening their treasures they offered unto him gifts, gold and frankincense and myrrh.*

LUKE 2:17, *And when they saw it, they made known concerning the saying which was spoken to them about this child.*

DURING the first three weeks of December most people give a lot of thought to what they want for Christmas. Little children's heads are crammed with images of the many things they want Santa Claus to bring them. Christmas shoppers scan their lists of relatives and friends and try to select just the gift they feel that each will want. But whether the giver's intuition be right or wrong, each person who is expecting to receive a gift knows quite clearly what he wants most of all. We can never be certain just how our Christmas planning and striving to please will turn out. All we can be certain of is that our big, bustling, commercialized Christmas will swell the charge accounts to alarming proportions!

In all of this self-centered Christmas anticipation, there is one other thought that should not be completely crowded out, namely, What does Christ want for Christmas? Place all the people in one group who think almost entirely of what THEY want for Christmas, and all the people in another group who think seriously of what CHRIST wants for Christmas and you will have an amazing contrast in the size of the groups. Yet, believe it or not, Christmas is the birthday of Christ, and He is the One Who is supremely entitled to our birthday presents. Is it not true that as Christians we should chiefly concern ourselves with what Christ wants for Christmas?

I. Christ Wants Our Worship.

The Nativity story is an 'open letter' to the world telling what Christ wants for Christmas. Any one who reads this 'open letter' will discover that what Christ wants most of all is our worship. This is plainly revealed on every page of the Christmas story. The proclamations of the angels, the homage of the shepherds, the adoration of Mary and Joseph, the benedictions of Elizabeth, Zacharias, Simeon and Anna, the worship of the Wise-men all point to this outstanding truth. The devout characters who participate in the Nativity drama, and all of its moving scenes combine to emphasize this central fact of the adoration and worship of the new-born King. This is not accidental. Not by any means. Rather it is God's carefully planned message to the world. It is God's way of telling us and all mankind what He wants first of all and last of all for His only begotten and well beloved Son. The Nativity story unfolds as a series of dramatized object lessons teaching the sublime truth that the Christ of God desires the homage, adoration and worship of all mankind. This is the lesson that comes home to our hearts whenever and wherever the Christmas story is clearly told. Our pageants, tableaus, dramas and exercises centering in the Manger of Bethlehem bring out this truth. However simply they may be presented they never fail to grip us with their moving appeal to reverence and worship the lowly Jesus. The masterpieces of inspiration and devotion in the world of art have the same effect upon us. The Christmas carols sing this message into our souls. The hymn, "O come, all ye faithful" strikes this chord in its grand refrain: "O come, let us adore Him, Christ the Lord." And the hymn, "Angels from the realms of glory" has perhaps the most satisfying refrain of all:

> "Come and worship, come and worship,
> Worship Christ, the new-born King!"

The visit of the Wise-men dramatizes this truth so beautifully and effectively that none may fail to understand it. "And they came into the house and saw the young child with Mary his mother; and they fell down and worshipped him." This story is perfectly amazing in its simplicity and compelling power. How many myriads of people it has brought to worship the Christ only God can know. Just two things are stated concerning these mysterious travellers from the East: they worshipped the Christ-child, and they offered Him their gifts. Everything else is left out of the picture. We are not told how many Wise-men there were; how they were dressed; how old they were; or what they said. There is not the faintest description of the scene other than their act of worship. Nothing is said about the house in which the Holy Family were staying. No description of the room in which they found the Christ-child is given. We are not told just how the child Jesus was presented to them, whether He was in His Mother's arms, lying in a bed, or moving about the house. The record simply states that "they fell down and worshipped him; and . . . offered unto him gifts." That is all we need to know. That is the lesson God wants us to learn. He wants us to bow in adoration and worship before His greatest gift of love to men.

As our knowledge of Christ transcends the knowledge the Wise-men had of Him, so our worship should be more freely and whole-heartedly rendered. We cannot tell how much the Wise-men knew concerning Him Who was born "King of the Jews." We do not know whether they ever received in their own country the Gospel news of His later life and ministry. At any rate, their knowledge of the significance of His birth at the time they came to Bethlehem must have been very fragmentary. And yet they devoutly worshipped Him and offered Him their best gifts. We have every opportunity to know the full revelation concerning Jesus' Person and His redeeming work. We know the story of His matchless life of holiness and loving deeds. We know how He died for us on Calvary's cross. We know how He rose from Joseph's tomb on Easter morning; how He was seen of those who loved Him; how He ascended into heaven, and how He promised to come again. It is ours then to worship Him as Jesus the Saviour, Christ the Lord, our Prophet, Priest and King. It is ours to remember that "God highly exalted him, and gave unto him the name which is above every name; that in the name of Jesus every knee should bow . . . and that every tongue should confess that Jesus Christ is Lord, to the glory of God the Father."

II. Christ Wants Our Gifts.

Enshrined in the Christmas story is the truth that Christ wants our gifts. Again the example of the Wise-men is given for our inspiration and guidance. "And opening their treasures they offered unto him gifts, gold and frankincense and myrrh." A very special significance attaches to these offerings of the Wise-men from the East. For one thing, the gifts which are three in number, provide the only clue we have as to the number of the Wise-men. The gifts of gold, frankincense and myrrh were evidently specimens of the products of their own country, and as such expressed the homage of their country to the new-found King. Furthermore, these princely worshippers were representatives of the Gentile world, hence their offerings symbolized the tribute of the entire heathen world to Christ. The Church has seen a profound symbolism in these three gifts. The gift of gold is emblematic of Christ's Royalty. He is the King of Kings and Lord of Lords. The gift of frankincense symbolizes His Deity, and reminds us that as the Son of God He is entitled to the homage and worship of all. The gift of myrrh is the symbol of His true Humanity, and points especially to His death and burial. It is similar to Mary's gift of costly ointment, concerning which Jesus said, "She hath anointed my body beforehand for the burying." Thus God used the tribute of the Wise-men to the infant Saviour to fulfill the word of prophecy, "And nations shall come to thy light, and kings to the brightness of thy rising." Their coming is also a further prophecy of the universal homage that would come to Him as the ages rolled on.

In the light of this example it is timely for us to inquire into the nature of real Christmas giving. It goes without saying that the vast bulk of our Christmas giving is not giving at all, but merely Christmas exchanging. It does not represent the sacrificial spirit of Christian giving and it does not promote the purposes of the Kingdom of God. I know a family, the members of which, in the days before the gold was called in by the government, used to give each other five dollar gold pieces for Christmas. One member would give out, say, five of the gold pieces, but he would receive in turn as many pieces as he had given. This nice exchange of gifts gave a lot of pleasure to every one, but in the end each one had just what he had started with. I do not know how perfect their Christmas joy would have been if one of the members had failed to put his gold pieces into circulation.

However thoughtful and nice the custom of exchanging gifts at Christmas may be, the fact remains that the great proportion of our giving is not upon the high plane of sacrificial Christian giving at all. The Wise-men gave their gifts to the Christ-child. *They did not expect any gift in return!* These valuable gifts were probably utilized by Mary and Joseph in defraying the expenses of their sojourn in Egypt in order to save the Child's life. If the gifts we bestow cost us something, and if they are used to help people and to enrich life, then Christ may bless them. But if they are given in a selfish, bargaining spirit, then they do not measure up to the standard of true Christmas giving. Those who have best interpreted the meaning of real Christmas giving have made it plain that we give to Christ when we make some sacrifice to help our fellowmen. This is the theme of such beautiful Christmas stories as Raymond Alden's "Why the Chimes Rang" and Henry van Dyke's "The Other Wise Man." The Other Wise Man found the King in using his treasures for the relief and succor of those in distress and need. How much of present day Christmas giving partakes of the spirit of Henry van Dyke's "Artaban" and of Alden's "little brother" it is not for us to say. But if we really want to know what Christ wants for Christmas, we can only make the discovery by consecrating our best gifts to Him and to His service.

What are the gifts that Christ wants from us? We can best answer this question by considering what kind of gifts Christ brings to us. Our Christmas giving is largely in the sphere of commercial and material things. The gifts Christ brings to human souls are spiritual gifts: love, peace, joy, mercy, forgiveness, purity, humility, faith. He had no material gifts to give, although the whole world was made through Him. When He died, He had only His seamless robe to leave in the hands of His crucifiers. But such were the infinite riches of His person, His character, His words, His deeds that the whole world has been blessed by His life. As Paul says, "For ye know the grace of our Lord Jesus Christ, that, though he was rich, yet for your sakes he became poor, that ye through his poverty might become rich." If Christ were to name the gifts He wants most of all from each one of us He would ask for the love and devotion of our hearts and for our lives freely given in His service for our fellowmen.

"These Be The Gifts" is the title of a poem by Grace Noll Crowell which strikes the key-note of genuine Christmas giving:

> "For the sake of the little Child of Bethlehem
> Who came to show compassion, and to bring
> The Bread of Life to every hungry heart,
> The Living Water to each thirsty thing,

Let us be kind today, as He is kind;
Let us be thoughtful of the hurt and sad;
Let us live simply as He lived, and Oh,
Let us walk humbly now, and let us be glad!

For the sake of one small Child we must be strong
And brave to follow where His footsteps lead:
Across a darkened land, along strange roads,
Through briars and storms to meet a hurt world's need.
These be the gifts to bring the gentle Christ:
This be the gold and incense we should take:
Our adoration, reverence and love;
Our lives—and freely spend them for His sake."

III. Christ Wants Our Witness.

Luke's story of the visit of the shepherds impresses upon us the truth that Christ wants our witness. The shepherds abiding in the fields heard the message and the music of the angels, then they hastened into the town of Bethlehem to see this thing that had come to pass. And so they were the first to find "Mary and Joseph, and the babe lying in the manger." "And when they saw it, they made known concerning the saying which was spoken to them about this child." The mother kept their sweet and wonderful words concerning her new-born babe, "pondering them in her heart." And later she became one of the chief witnesses to her Son and Lord, for it was she who gave the story of His birth to the world. All the other people about Bethlehem and vicinity who heard the glad tidings of great joy from the lips of the shepherds were filled with awe and wonder. The shepherds returned to their homes and sheepfolds glorifying and praising God for all the things they had heard and seen. And ever afterward they found great joy in telling the story exactly as it had been spoken unto them.

"Ye shall be my witnesses," says the Lord and Master to all of His disciples. And He means that we shall begin just where we are. He wants us to tell the story in our own homes; in our own churches; in our own communities, and to take it to the uttermost parts of the earth. The best way for us to be faithful witnesses is to live as He lived, and to tell the Gospel story even as God has made it known unto us in His Son.

WHEN THE ANGELS WENT AWAY

All My Heart This Night Rejoices

All my heart this night rejoices,
As I hear, far and near,
Sweetest angel voices;
"Christ is born," their choirs are singing,
Till the air everywhere
Now with joy is ringing.

Hark! a voice from yonder manger,
Soft and sweet, doth entreat:
"Flee from woe and danger;
Brethren, come; from all doth grieve you
You are freed; all you need
I will surely give you."

Come, then, let us hasten yonder:
Here let all, great and small,
Kneel in awe and wonder;
Love Him who with love is yearning,
Hail the Star that from afar
Bright with hope is burning.

Blessed Saviour, let me find Thee;
Keep Thou me close to Thee,
Cast me not behind Thee:
Life of life, my heart Thou stillest,
Calm I rest on Thy breast,
All this void Thou fillest.
—Rev. Paul Gerhardt, 1653.

Trans. by Catherine Winkworth, 1858.

XII

When the Angels Went Away

LUKE 2:15, *And it came to pass, when the angels went away from them into heaven, the shepherds said one to another, Let us now go even unto Bethlehem, and see this thing that is come to pass, which the Lord has made known unto us.*

THERE is a phrase in the story of the Angels and the Shepherds that we have all read many times, and yet we have probably passed over it without thinking of its deep and hidden meaning. I refer to the phrase of five words, *"when the angels went away."* For the angels did go away again into heaven. Their appearance to the shepherds was a real event and their disappearance was likewise a fact of reality.

Much as we would like to live continuously upon the high plane of spiritual exultation and beatific joy, the fact remains that this experience is not granted to mortals. The angels go away. Their music fades from the skies. The heavens become silent again. The glory of the Lord shines no more. Night on the plains of Bethlehem becomes like all the other myriad thousands of nights that have brooded over the City of David—all save one.

But after all, the strange and wonderful events of Holy Night are in accord with the facts of life and of our spiritual world. Every grand climax must be followed by an anti-climax. Every great action must produce its corresponding reaction. Music has its crescendo and its diminuendo. Art has its light and shade. Nature has its day and night; its sunshine and clouds; its summer and winter. Life has its joys and sorrows; its smiles and tears; its glad meetings and its sad partings. So it is quite in keeping with the Divine plan for human life that the Christmas angels should go away again into heaven. The herald angel stood by the shepherds and delivered to them his message. Then he departed, as any

115

'messenger boy' will do after he has delivered a telegram. The angelic hosts suddenly appeared in the skies, gave their hymn of glory and of peace, and went away as suddenly as they came. What does God have to say to us in these wistful words: "when the angels went away from them into heaven"?

I. God Has Sent a Message to the World.

The departure of the angel-messengers reminds us that God has sent a message to the world. The thing of supreme importance in connection with their coming is the message they bring. Having delivered the message their mission is performed. They go away again into heaven to render other service for the Lord of Hosts. The angels do not stay to call attention to themselves. They do not occupy the center of the stage in the Nativity drama. Their message is the 'Prologue' and when this is spoken their part is finished. They herald the coming of Another Who is "so much better than the angels," and Who "hath inherited a more excellent name than they" (Hebrews 1:4). By their withdrawal they give place to this Superior Personage; they emphasize the dignity of His character; they indicate that their heaven-sent message is fulfilled in Him.

The message of the angels is a very simple one. It can be reduced to a single word. We are told that General Bramwell Booth was once asked to cable a message from England to the Salvation Army in America on some important occasion. He cabled the one word, "OTHERS". If we want to know what message the angels of God brought to the world when Jesus was born we will find it in the one word, "SAVIOUR". The angels spoke of the "good tidings of great joy" to all the people, but these good tidings concerned Him Who was born in the city of David a Saviour, Christ the Lord. The heavenly host sang their hymn of glory to God in heaven, but this was in praise of God for the Saviour He had sent to the world. They also sang of peace on earth and good will among men, but this was in honor of the Saviour for the blessings of peace and love He would bring to the hearts of men. There is only one meaning we can take from heaven's message to the shepherds at Christmas time: it is all summed up in Him Who is the Saviour, Christ the Lord.

The message concerning the Saviour is the all important fact of Christmas. And this message comes direct from God by way of accrediting and approving the mission of His Son. This word of divine ordination and approval came to Jesus at various times during His public ministry. As He took His place in the line of those who were coming to be baptized of John in the Jordan He thus indicated that He came to be identified with sinners and to take upon Himself the burden of their sin. At this time God set His seal of approval upon the Saviourhood of Jesus, for "the heavens were opened unto him, and he saw the Spirit of God descending as a dove, and coming upon him; and lo, a voice out of the heavens, saying, This is my beloved Son, in whom I am well pleased." Again, as Jesus conversed with Moses and Elijah about the offering up of Himself in Jerusalem, He was transfigured by a holy radiance and a voice out of the cloud was heard, saying, "This is my beloved Son, in whom I am well pleased; hear ye him." Also at the time the Greeks came to Him in the temple, our Lord's acceptance of His passion as the only way of glorifying His Father was sanctioned by a voice from heaven saying, "I have both glorified it, and will glorify it again." God has spoken through prophets and angels, through His Son, and by direct means to the effect that Jesus came to be the Saviour of mankind.

No man can know the meaning of Christmas therefore unless he has accepted Christ as his personal Saviour. Those who fail to receive Him as Saviour turn deaf ears to the holy, majestic and sovereign voice of God. The loving Father gave His Son because all men need a Saviour. He has graciously provided the means of salvation and eternal life for all who will repent of their sins and turn to Christ as their Redeemer and Saviour. Let us be sure that we receive the message of the angels and hearken to the majestic voice of Him Who has glorified His Son through death and resurrection.

II. God Has Given a Commission to His Servants.

Again, the withdrawal of the angels into heaven reminds us that God has given a commission to His servants. When the angels went away the shepherds immediately found there was something for them to do. They had seen the light, they had heard the message, they had received the sign. Now they must act quickly upon the revelation that had come to them. And so they did. They said one to another, "Let us now go even unto Bethlehem, and see this thing that is come to pass, which the Lord has made known unto us." And millions of hearts the world around have dwelt with love and reverence upon what they found when they came to the place where there was a manger.

The shepherds responded to the message of the angels in just the way God wants all people to respond. They received the message into their hearts, believed it and acted upon it. And when they had verified all that the angel had spoken, they made known to others the whole story of God's revelation to them. Even so the solemn voice of duty comes to every soul that has heard the Christmas story. Each one who receives the Saviour is commissioned to tell others about Him. The angels proclaimed His birth, but the task of spreading the good news around the world has been committed to men. The angels go away to tell us their task is completed and ours is begun. We cannot keep Christmas ourselves unless we share its message with others. Christmas, rightly understood, is a great challenge to bestir ourselves to fresh evangelistic zeal and to greater Kingdom service. We dare not be completely satisfied with our own joys and pleasures that center around Christmas as though this were all there is to it. We must remember what God wants us to do in forwarding His plans and purposes in Christ. We must make haste, as did the faithful shepherds of Bethlehem, to be about the business of our King. Only as we do this can the deepest joy and peace of Christmas come to us.

We live in a world that needs above all else the Gospel of the Saviour of men. Whatever opinions may be current about the faults and failures of the Church, the fact remains that Almighty God has given His Son to be the only Saviour from sin. And all those who have truly found Him know that He is an all sufficient Saviour. It is the duty and privilege of all who have so found Him to give a clear, earnest and unfailing testimony to His wonderful power and saving love. While countless numbers of people are cold and indifferent to Christ and give evidence that they have not heard the good news of the angel-herald as the shepherds heard it, yet it is the duty of all believers to let their light shine before men to the glory of their Saviour. Our only hope of salvation, immortality and eternal life is in Christ Jesus. The only hope of the world is in Him, and to Him we must bring those who will be saved.

III. God Has Revealed the Secret of Keeping Christmas.

Lastly, the disappearance of the angels should teach us that God has revealed the secret of how we may keep Christmas as an abiding experience. The angels went away from the shepherds, but the shepherds had Christmas in their hearts. They no longer needed the objective sight of the shining ones nor the sound of their heavenly voices. They had the message and the music in their hearts, and their eyes had seen the infant Saviour, God's little Lamb Who was to be the Shepherd of Israel. We may be absolutely sure that those shepherds never forgot the experience of that Holy Night; that they never lost the new-found joy and peace that came to them with the finding of the Saviour.

We all know full well how the objective things that make Christmas a happy occasion soon pass away. Loved ones who have been brought together in happy reunion are separated again. The feasting and the merry-making are over. The lights are taken from the Christmas trees. The turkey carcasses, white and clean as the Valley of Dry Bones, are thrown out. The toys are broken. The neckties are exchanged for some we can wear. The things that remain are the happy memories and the bills to be paid over the next few months. All these things go into the making of a Merry Christmas, but these alone will not enable us to keep Christmas with us in the days to come.

Those who observe Christmas merely in a superficial manner soon find that the sky is silent, the music is hushed, the light is gone. When it is all over they have received no spiritual uplift nor lasting peace. The angels go away and there is nothing left to take their place. But those who seek and find the deeper meaning of Christmas in fellowship with Christ Jesus the Lord have a profound spiritual experience which they keep ever afterward. There is a beautiful old English custom of lighting the Yule Log from a fragment of the Log left from the year before. Thus in a symbolic way, the Christmas that is past and gone serves to light up the Christmas which is to be. If we keep Christmas in the truly spiritual sense it leaves an invaluable residue with us that makes for a richer and fuller Christmas ahead. Our experience of Christmas then becomes like the experience of Mary of Bethany as she sat at Jesus' feet and heard His word. In commenting upon her wise procedure the Master said, "Mary hath chosen the good part, which shall not be taken away from her." In this connection we may also recall that this was essentially the experience of Christmas that came to Mary the mother of Jesus. The record is that "Mary kept all these sayings, pondering them in her heart." If we keep the Christmas message in our hearts and ponder reverently over its meaning, we will have something which shall not be taken away from us. Let us too choose the good part.

From whatever angle we approach the story of the first Christmas, we see that it was essentially a simple, quiet, calm and peaceful event. Where there was bustling and confusion, as in the Bethlehem inn, Christ was crowded out. Where there was wicked envy, ill-will and worldly pleasure, as in the palace of Herod, no glad tidings of great joy were brought. Christmas as it is generally observed to-day is essentially a complex, busy, blustering celebration. We have a popular phrase that describes it exactly—"the Christmas rush." It is just that. As a result, multitudes of busy, overburdened people have no time to possess their own souls or to meditate quietly and serenely upon the sweet wonders and peace-giving messages of the birth of Christ. When Christmas truly comes to a person, it comes as a deep and abiding spiritual experience. Life is opened to messages from heaven, celestial music is heard, visions of things invisible and eternal are seen. A comforting sense of the presence of God-with-us is felt. Light is given for the way ahead, and the star of hope gleams brighter and more fair.

Perhaps it is timely to take stock of ourselves and to consider exactly what Christmas has meant to us; what it has left with us. Aside from the objective and material things it has brought to us, has it left in our souls a richer experience of God in Christ, a deeper peace, a fuller joy? When the angels go away from our sight, do we know that they have gone into heaven; that they are still there to watch over us and to minister to our needs? If we have learned to know the redeeming love of God in Christ, if we have found a deep inner peace and joy, if we have learned to trust in God's protecting goodness and care, then we have learned the secret of keeping Christmas as an abiding experience in our souls.

AFTER CHRISTMAS

Hail to the Lord's Anointed

Hail to the Lord's Anointed,
   Great David's greater Son!
Hail, in the time appointed,
   His reign on earth begun!
He comes to break oppression,
   To set the captive free,
To take away transgression,
   And rule in equity.

He shall come down like showers
   Upon the fruitful earth;
And love, joy, hope, like flowers,
   Spring in His path to birth;
Before Him on the mountains
   Shall peace, the herald, go,
And righteousness, in fountains,
   From hill to valley flow.

Kings shall fall down before Him,
   And gold and incense bring;
All nations shall adore Him,
   His praise all people sing;
For Him shall prayer unceasing
   And daily vows ascend;
His kingdom still increasing,
   A kingdom without end.

O'er every foe victorious,
   He on His throne shall rest,
From age to age more glorious,
   All blessing and all-blest:
The tide of time shall never
   His covenant remove,
His Name shall stand for ever,—
   That Name to us is Love.

        —JAMES MONTGOMERY, 1821.

XIII

After Christmas

MATTHEW 2:14, *And he arose and took the young child and his mother by night and departed into Egypt.*

THE Apostle Paul wrote in his last letter to Timothy, "Every scripture inspired of God is also profitable for teaching, for reproof, for correction, for instruction which is in righteousness." Athanasius has said, "All Divine Scripture is a teacher of true virtue and faith." This is incontestably true of the passage in Matthew's Gospel which follows the account of the birth of Jesus and the visit of the Wise-men. The passage in question tells of the flight of the Holy Family into Egypt, and of Herod's cruel slaughter of the infants of Bethlehem.

It is customary at Christmas time to center our attention upon the narratives in Matthew and Luke that tell of the Saviour's birth. After Christmas we turn to thoughts of the New Year. As a result, the narratives in the Gospels that tell us of what happened immediately after Christmas are ignored and forgotten. I cannot recall ever having heard a sermon on The Flight Into Egypt or on The Slaughter of the Innocents. Nor are these themes given a conspicuous part in the pageantry, the drama, the story, or the music that seek to commemorate the Christmas message. But as we turn to these subjects as an after-Christmas meditation we find they contain much that is "profitable for teaching, for reproof, for correction, for instruction which is in righteousness."

I. The Fact of Divine Guidance and Protection.

Three facts of profound significance are brought out in the story of the flight into Egypt. The first is the fact of divine guidance and protection in the case of Joseph's family. This truth has been clearly evident in the Christmas story. The Wise-men were the objects of divine guidance and protection on their journeys to and from

Bethlehem. The shepherds were also guided to Bethlehem by supernatural signs. In these after-Christmas events we see the same
over-ruling Providence at work guiding and protecting the Holy
Family during these crucial days. Three times in this brief narrative we are told that an angel of the Lord appeared to Joseph in a
dream and instructed him what to do. Straightway after the Wise-
men had departed into their own country, and before the wily
Herod had a chance to act, an angel of the Lord appeared to Joseph
and instructed him to flee into Egypt in order to escape the plot
Herod was forming to destroy the young Child. This instruction
was very definite. Joseph was told not only to flee, but to flee into
Egypt and to remain there until he should receive further instruction. Joseph arose that same night and took the young child and
his mother and departed into Egypt where they sojourned until
Herod was dead. Their sojourn in Egypt could not have been
long, for Herod died soon after Jesus was born, and the child is still
spoken of as "a young child" when Joseph returned into the land
of Israel. After the death of Herod, the angel appeared to Joseph in
Egypt and bade him return to the land of Israel, saying, "they are
dead that sought the young child's life." Joseph straightway obeyed
and returned to the land of Israel, intending to take up his abode in
Bethlehem. But when he learned that Archelaus, the son of Herod
the Great, was reigning in his father's stead, he was afraid to enter
his domain. His caution is readily explained when we remember
that Archelaus had inaugurated his bloody reign by slaughtering
3,000 Jews within the sacred precincts of the temple itself. Again
Joseph was warned by God in a dream and instructed to take up
his residence in Nazareth of Galilee.

In connection with this fact of divine guidance and protection,
we have the corresponding fact of Joseph's obedience to and co-operation with the divine will. How superbly admirable does the
character of Joseph appear in this whole story! With what noble
humility, stedfastness, and loving solicitude does he perform the
role of father and shepherd in relation to his sacred charge! He appears throughout as the heaven-appointed guardian, the divinely-
instructed sentinel set to watch over the helpless infant days of the
Son of the Most High. It was a noble role, and he played his part
well. Perhaps few people have been able to appreciate the delicacy
of the situation in which Joseph found himself. He was not the

holy Child's real father, but nevertheless we see him bestowing the tenderest fatherly love and care upon the Child, and the most understanding marital affection upon the cherished wife and mother. The devout and godly man submits himself as an obedient servant of the divine will and instantly co-operates with the divine purposes as they are revealed to him. God invariably chooses to work through those who already have personal qualifications for the service He desires them to render. And so here. Joseph was eminently fitted by his life of true piety and fellowship with God, his large and loving nature, his spirit of resourcefulness, and his watchful and tender solicitude for the well being of others to serve as the heaven-sent guardian of the infant Saviour. We know very little of Joseph's later life. We know only that he was a carpenter at Nazareth. But the important thing is that he fulfilled the high mission of his life, namely, that of protecting the mother and the young Child from wicked men who sought to do them harm.

God needs men and women to-day who are as faithfully devoted to the interests of His Son as was the foster-parent Joseph. Oftentimes the cause of Christ suffers injury because His followers fail to be watchful and vigilant; because they neglect to be solicitous for the highest interests of His Kingdom. Every Christian should consider himself a heaven-sent guardian and shepherd of Christ's flock. If we fail to discharge our sacred obligation, the Church of Christ suffers by so much. This is one of the after-Christmas lessons that applies to each one of us all the year round.

II. The Fact of Fulfilled Prophecy.

The second great fact in the story of the flight into Egypt is the fulfilment of inspired prophecy. Matthew's Gospel is pre-eminently the Gospel of Fulfilment. In the present case, three different events are said to have prophetic significance. First, the fact that Joseph and Mary came up out of Egypt with the child Jesus is said to confirm the prophetic utterance of Hosea, "Out of Egypt did I call my Son." The background of this prophecy is the historical fact of Israel's exodus from Egypt under the leadership of Moses. But the prophecy also signified that just as Israel came out of Egypt as a young nation, so the Messiah would come out of Egypt as a young child.

Matthew then declares that the weeping of the mothers of Bethlehem over their slaughtered babies was a fulfillment of the prophecy of Jeremiah, saying,

> "A voice was heard in Ramah,
> Weeping and great mourning,
> Rachel weeping for her children;
> And she would not be comforted, because they are not."

This prophecy referred primarily to the mourning of Israel over the taking of a large portion of the tribes of Benjamin and Judah as captives to Babylon. In describing the bitter grief that filled the land, Jeremiah imagines the long-buried Rachel, the mother of Benjamin, arising from her grave to mourn the captivity of her children. Rachel's tomb stood close to Bethlehem, and now another bitter woe had come upon the land in the ruthless slaughter of the innocents of Bethlehem. Accordingly, Matthew sees another fulfillment of Jeremiah's prophecy in the wailing of the bereft mothers, and again Rachel is represented as arising from her grave to weep over her slaughtered children.

Joseph's return to Galilee and establishment in Nazareth is likewise declared to be a fulfillment of the prophecy concerning Jesus that "he should be called a Nazarene." There is no specific prophecy in these words to be found in the Old Testament. But there are many prophecies that give the same meaning. The term 'Nazarene' was a term of reproach. "Can any good thing come out of Nazareth?" asked Nathanael of Philip. So the prophecy of Isaiah that the Messiah was to be despised and rejected of men accords with Matthew's declaration. Matthew's statement means that the general tendency of prophecy was to describe the Messiah as one who would be despised and rejected of men, in other words, a Nazarene.

From these examples of fulfilled prophecy we may properly infer that God's purposes are in the process of fulfillment in all human history. Again and again that which was predicted centuries before, came to pass when the fulness of times was come. That this is true of Bible history no right thinking person would care to deny. But if this has been the true interpretation of ancient history, why is it not equally true of modern history? Our God is the same yesterday, to-day and for ever. We have every reason to believe that God is carrying out His purposes in the lives of individuals and nations to-day just as He did in the life of Joseph and in the history of Israel. Tennyson's great affirmation in "Locksley Hall" is certainly true:

"Yet I doubt not thro' the ages one increasing purpose runs,
And the thoughts of men are widen'd with the process of the suns."

Of course there are no written or recorded prophecies concerning our lives. The future remains unknown to us. The members of our high school graduating classes are in the habit of writing prophecies concerning what is to happen to each member in the future, but these predictions are more famed for their wit than for their accuracy. Although we have no reliable predictions concerning our future, yet the fact remains that God's plans and purposes are being fulfilled in all of our lives. He has some wise and good plan for the life of each one of His children. His guiding hand is over all; His providential care is the portion of His people; His lovingkindness is new every morning, and His faithfulness every night. All that is required for the highest blessedness of our lives is that we shall co-operate with the divine plan, and readily submit our lives to His leading and care.

It is a source of infinite comfort and joy to know that He will go with us into the New Year, and will watch over us all the days of our lives. Yea, though we walk through the valley of the shadow of death, we need fear no evil: for He is with us; His rod and His staff they comfort us. Surely goodness and mercy shall follow us all the days of our lives: and we will dwell in the house of the Lord for ever.

III. The Fact of Rejection.

The third thing in this story is the grim fact of the rejection of the Son of God. The fact of rejection in this case is crystallized in the murderous attempt of king Herod to destroy the Christ-child. The unspeakably cruel and heartless deed of Herod in slaughtering the children of Bethlehem accords well with what we know of his infamous character. His long reign of thirty-four years as king of Judea had been darkened by similar acts of bloodshed. He was not a real Jew but an Idumean, and he had obtained the throne by conquest. He was hated as a vile usurper of the throne by the Jews. He was exceedingly suspicious of members of his own family whom he thought might displace him on the throne. And his bloody method was to murder anyone who appeared to be a rival for his kingdom. Only a few years before the birth of Jesus, Herod had murdered his own sons, Alexander and Aristobulus, by having them strangled. And just a few days before he died, he had another son, Antipater, put to death for conspiring against him. When Jesus was born, Herod was about seventy years old, and was in the last year of his evil life. He was slowly dying of a dreadful malady, and he was little better than a madman, having suffered the tortures of remorse for the murder of his once beloved wife, Mariamne.

When the Wise-men from the east came to Jerusalem and inquired concerning him who was born "King of the Jews", there was just one thought that absorbed Herod's crafty mind, namely, how to be rid at once of this suspected rival to the throne. And so the bloodthirsty tyrant sent forth his minions to slaughter all the male children from two years old and under in Bethlehem and the borders thereof. This was not as large a massacre as some have thought. There were probably not more than twenty children in all. But what has the number to do with it? Imagine the brutal soldiers coming into your own home, and seizing your own child out of the mother's struggling arms, and heartlessly slaying the beautiful little baby before the mother's horror-stricken eyes. But God was watching over His own Child, and had sent Him away from the evil clutches of Herod. He had given His holy angels charge over Him to keep Him in all His ways.

These little children of Bethlehem have been called the "protomartyrs" of Christianity, and again "the blossom of martyrdom". They were the first of the long line of Christian martyrs whose blood is the seed of the Church. They were the first to bear the wrath of the iniquitous and unbelieving world of men who were to reject the Son of God and array themselves in hostile opposition to His Church. "A sword shall pierce through thine own soul," said the inspired Simeon to Mary in the temple. And the first sharp thrust of that sword was felt when Mary learned of the Bethlehem tragedy. How her mother heart must have been drawn to those grief-stricken mothers who had thus innocently suffered for her sake!

Thus the grim truth of the Saviour's rejection appears at once. And throughout the history of the Church, the bright picture of the

Saviour's love has been thrown against the dark background of His rejection by the wicked and unbelieving world.

But we must not forget that those babies who died for the child Jesus are saved by Him, and will be restored to their mother's arms in the resurrection at the last day. The prophet who told of Rachel's weeping for her children also says in the verses that immediately follow that Rachel should be comforted. "Thus saith Jehovah: Refrain thy voice from weeping, and thine eyes from tears; for thy work shall be rewarded, saith Jehovah; and they shall come again from the land of the enemy. And there is hope for thy latter end, saith Jehovah; and thy children shall come again to their own border."

Thus the meaning of Christmas to those who are united with Christ will persist throughout time and eternity. There is nothing that a hostile, unbelieving world can do to separate us from the love of God, which is in Christ Jesus our Lord. We are assured of His divine guidance and protection; of the fulfillment of His gracious purposes in our lives; of our acceptance in the Beloved, an acceptance that issues in the eternal life of the resurrection and the heavenly Kingdom.

CHRISTMAS TEARS

O Thou! Who by a Star Didst Guide

O Thou! who by a star didst guide
　The wise men on their way,
Until it came and stood beside
　The place where Jesus lay;

Although by stars Thou dost not lead
　Thy servants now below,
Thy Holy Spirit, when they need,
　Will show them how to go.

As yet we know Thee but in part;
　But still we trust Thy word,
That blessed are the pure in heart,
　For they shall see the Lord.

O Saviour! give us, then, Thy grace,
　To make us pure in heart;
That we may see Thee face to face
　Hereafter, as Thou art.

　　　　　　　　—JOHN MASON NEALE.

XIV

Christmas Tears

LUKE 2:34-35, *And Simeon blessed them, and said unto Mary, his mother, Behold, this child is set for the falling and the rising of many in Israel; and for a sign which is spoken against; yea and a sword shall pierce through thine own soul; that thoughts out of many hearts may be revealed.*

C HRISTMAS is pre-eminently the time of "Joy to the world", and we like to make the most of this happy note. Our favorite Christmas greeting is "Merry Christmas" and we add to that a sincere wish for a "Happy New Year." We thoughtfully build our plans and hopes so that Christmas will bring the fullest possible measure of joy to the greatest number. Back of all the careful planning and busy preparation in a million homes is the thought of joy that will come to the children on Christmas morning. Christmas visits, family reunions, friendly gatherings and numerous other phases of the festive occasion are planned in the hope of bringing new joy and gladness to the circle of relatives and friends to which we belong. The spirit of charitable and sacrificial giving which abounds has for its aim the bringing of joy and happiness to poor children and needy men and women. May the real joy of Christmas be spread abroad in the land until it touches every home and every life!

But life is not all joy. Hence Christmas cannot be all joy for all people. Sorrow is never very far away from joy. Sorrow and joy are almost like the two sides of a coin. Christmas may be all joy for multitudes of happy, carefree children, but it will inevitably have other meanings for those who are older in years and experience. This is as it should be, and we need not be afraid of the sorrows, disappointments and tears that creep unbidden into our lives and become intermingled with our Christmas joys. These experiences, rightly received and understood, will serve to deepen and sanctify the real joy of Christmas.

It is not our purpose to detract one iota from the joy of Christmas in dealing with the unusual theme which we have chosen. Rather it is our hope that by recognizing the darker side of the picture we will succeed in throwing into brighter relief the unfailing joy of the true Christmas experience. The Gospel of God's love would be very incomplete indeed if we could not find comfort, hope and joy in spite of or rather because of Christmas Tears.

I. Christmas a Time of Precious Memories.

Christmas tears will moisten the eyes and cheeks of some by reason of the flood of memories that come thronging back. For those who are older Christmas is a time of many memories. For the most part it is a time of happy memories. Each succeeding Christmas is connected in thought with all the other Christmases that are past and gone. There are memories of our childhood Christmases in our parents' home, with our brothers and sisters who shared the happy delights and surprises of those far-off days. We cannot recall them without being thankful to God and to our parents for giving us happy childhood memories. And yet these happy memories seem to have gathered to themselves certain other qualities with the passing of the years. As we look more closely, they seem to have a mellow, wistful aura about them that gives them a tinge of sadness. And if we take the time to dream a little, and to dwell upon those living images of the past we are very apt to find the tears coming to our eyes. For those days are gone for ever. The scenes have greatly changed. The old home no longer stands, or has fallen into the hands of strangers. Our parents may have been called to their Long Home. The brothers and sisters cannot be gathered together again. Our hearts have entered into the experience described by Thomas Moore in his wistful poem, "The Light of Other Days."

> "Oft in the stilly night
>   Ere slumber's chain has bound me,
> Fond Memory brings the light
>   Of other days around me:
>   The smiles, the tears
>   Of boyhood's years,
>   The words of love then spoken;

The eyes that shone,
Now dimm'd and gone,
The cheerful hearts now broken!
Thus in the stilly night
Ere slumber's chain has bound me
Sad Memory brings the light
Of other days around me.

When I remember all
The friends so link'd together
I've seen around me fall
Like leaves in wintry weather,
I feel like one
Who treads alone
Some banquet-hall deserted,
Whose lights are fled
Whose garlands dead,
And all but he departed!
Thus in the stilly night
Ere slumber's chain has bound me,
Sad Memory brings the light
Of other days around me."

Moreover, real experiences of sorrow and tears do come even at Christmas time. Many home circles have anniversaries of sorrow which cast their sobering influences over the whole season. Old familiar faces are no longer seen in the candlelight. The well remembered accents of their voices are not heard. Their comforting, sustaining presence is not felt. Of course Christmas can never be the same again with them away. Truly there are reasons known to many sad and lonely hearts for Christmas grief.

II. Christmas a Time of Tender Sympathies.

Christmas tears are bound to flow because for many it is a time of tender sympathies. To sympathize with a person is to suffer along with that person in his trial. Shakespeare gives us a dramatic example of true sympathy in the words of the noble Miranda in "The Tempest." She is speaking about the shipwreck:

"O! I have suffer'd
With those that I saw suffer: a brave vessel,
Who had, no doubt, some noble creature in her,
Dash'd all to pieces. O! the cry did knock
Against my very heart. Poor souls, they perish'd."

Especially at Christmas time the cries of a needy, sinful world do knock against the very hearts of Christ's servants. As we gain a fresh conception of God's goodness and love to the world in the gift of His Son, and as we come to possess a new hope that Christ's love and peace may prevail among men, we are bound to be moved by the old wrongs and sins and miseries that blight the lives of our fellowmen.

The Reverend George Matheson has said, "Every sympathy is a memory. I feel for you what at one time I felt for myself. The remembrance of my personal want is the measure of my sympathetic power. . . . It is not possible that sympathy for my brother man can precede my personal experience. All my compassions are echoes—echoes of the strains of sorrow I have heard in my own ear; omit the strain, and you remove the echo." To be truly sympathetic then, we must want for all other people what we want for ourselves. Do we want our own children to be happy and well provided for? Then we should want other children less fortunate than ours to share some of the good things of Christmas. Do we want our loved ones to be saved from the debauching carnalities and blasting evils of the wicked world? Then we should sympathize with those who have loved ones whose lives are broken and marred with the curse of drink and stained with the guilt of crime. Do we want to dwell in peace, each in his own humble home, where none shall make us afraid? Then we must have great sympathy for those whose lives and homes are ravaged and ruined by the horrors of war and bloodshed. Do we cherish the hope that all of our dear ones shall be safe in the fold of God, safe from the sins of the world, safe in the Saviour's love, safe for the heaven above? Surely then we will have compassion for the lost prodigals who are perishing with hunger as they feed upon the husks of the world, far from the Father's home.

As we think upon these grim realities in the light of the Christmas message of love, peace, joy, hope and salvation, how can we help weeping over the sins and sorrows and needless sufferings of our fellow human beings? Worldlings do not weep, because they are satisfied with the world as it is. But those who have caught the vision of God's purpose to build the Kingdom of Heaven upon this earth cannot avoid sorrow and tears at the long delay. But sympathy that vents itself in silly sentiment and vapid tears is not worthy of consideration. If our sympathy is real, we will do all in our power to make the world better; to help those in need; to do unto others as we would have others do unto us. We will not pass by on the other side with a self-righteous grunt: "They have only themselves to blame." We will not tie up our gift of sympathy in a napkin and hide it away in the earth, but we will put it to work in kind and helpful ministries to those in need. We will follow the Master; we will go on our way doing good.

III. Christmas a Time of Neglected Opportunities.

The chief reason for Christmas tears lies in the fact that Christmas is a time of neglected opportunities. This has been true from the beginning. It is true to-day. The saddest thing in the whole world is the fact of the rejection of the Son of God. This fact of rejection stands out boldly in the Nativity narrative as well as in the whole life story of Jesus. "He came unto his own, and they that were his own received him not." This continuing rejection of God's gift of love is the saddest fact history records. When we examine the words of Simeon to Mary we find this sad fact of rejection clearly indicated. "Behold, this child is set for the falling and the rising of many in Israel; and for a sign which is spoken against; yea and a sword shall pierce through thine own soul; that thoughts out of many hearts may be revealed." Surely there is enough here to bring tears to the mother's eyes! She could not understand all that was meant at the time, but as time passed the strange words of Simeon unfolded their tragic meaning.

We read the Christmas story to gain joy and hope and peace. But how can we read the *complete* story without finding reasons for sadness and grief? What mother can think of the trials Mary suffered in coming to Bethlehem and in being crowded out of a place of warmth, comfort and care without tender sympathy and tears? Who can think of those sorrowing mothers of Bethlehem who wept and wailed for their little ones so mercilessly slaughtered by the bloody king Herod without bitter grief? Surely the heart of

Mary would be broken with sorrow and anguish when she learned of those precious little martyrs who had died in the place of her Son. But the cup of her sorrow was filled to overflowing years later when she became the eye-witness of the crucifixion of her first-born Son. Then it was that the sword of anguish pierced through her own soul.

> "Beside the cross in tears
>   The woeful mother stood,
> Bent 'neath the weight of years,
>   And viewed His flowing blood;
> Her mind with grief was torn,
>   Her strength was ebbing fast,
> And through her heart forlorn
>   The sword of anguish passed."

The national opposition and rejection of their Messiah by the Jews is a matter of history. This is sad enough. But the tragedy continues in that Christ is still shut out of His rightful home in millions of hearts. The Gospel of Christmas is given to the world each year on the wings of song and story, but still the many do not receive the Christ. Millions of modern Jews continue to reject the Christ and so deny their own sacred Scriptures. Multitudes of Gentiles who have heard His name do not accept His salvation or own His way of life. He is crowded out of the political regimes of great nations; His program of peace and brotherhood, of love and good will, is blasted to bits by the frightful carnage of war. His own people, who have confessed His name and united with His visible body, the Church, often follow Him afar off. Many have turned back altogether and walk no more with Him. He stands knocking at the door of many a church, many a home, many a heart, but alas! there is no room for Him; He is still crowded out. Those who perceive the real spiritual meaning and opportunity of Christmas in God's offer of love, mercy and forgiveness to the world are bound to mourn at this blind and heartless rejection of the Saviour by the sinful, unbelieving world.

Jesus said, "Blessed are they that mourn: for they shall be comforted." Blessed are they who mourn in genuine sympathy for the homeless, wandering Christ Child. For those who thus weep at the heartless neglect, indifference and opposition of others, will at the same time long to receive and welcome the Christ Child into their own hearts and lives. Christmas comes with its tender appeal to all to receive the Christ, God's well beloved and only begotten Son. The promise is that as many as receive Him, to them God gives the right to become His children, members of His own family, children nourished, protected and cared for in the Father's household where Christ is the Son and elder Brother. If we want to bring Christmas joy in heaven instead of Christmas tears, we will receive the Christ Child as God's own gift of love to mankind. Our hearts will echo the sweet invitation of Martin Luther's song, "A Christmas Carol For Children":

> "Were earth a thousand times as fair,
> Beset with gold and jewels rare,
> She yet were far too poor to be
> A narrow cradle, Lord, for Thee.
>
> Ah, dearest Jesus, Holy Child!
> Make Thee a bed, soft, undefiled,
> Within my heart, that it may be
> A quiet chamber kept for Thee."

CHRISTMAS AND THE CROSS

The Sky Can Still Remember

The sky can still remember
  The earliest Christmas morn,
When in the cold December
  The Saviour Christ was born.
No star unfolds its glory,
  No trumpet wind is blown,
But tells the Christmas story
  In music of its own.

O never-failing splendor!
  O never-silent song!
Still keep the green earth tender,
  Still keep the gray earth strong,
Still keep the brave earth dreaming
  Of deeds that shall be done,
While children's lives come streaming
  Like sun-beams from the sun.

O angels sweet and splendid,
  Throng in our hearts and sing
The wonders which attended
  The coming of the King;
Till we too, boldly pressing
  Where once the shepherds trod,
Climb Bethlehem's Hill of Blessing,
  And find the Son of God.

      —BISHOP PHILLIPS BROOKS (1835-1893).

XV

Christmas and the Cross

MATTHEW 1:21, *And she shall bring forth a son; and thou shalt call his name JESUS; for it is he that shall save his people from their sins.*

W E DO not commonly connect Christmas and the Cross in our practical thinking. In fact, while we are under the magic spell of the gay and happy holiday season, we can readily sense a reluctance on the part of many to associate so bright a thing as Christmas with so grim a fact as Calvary. However this may be, as students of the complete Christmas message we should be willing to know the whole truth and eager to learn all the lessons God has set for us to learn in the Gospel of His Infant Son.

We do not need to force the issue in connecting Bethlehem with Jerusalem, the manger with the cross, His birth with His death. It is not necessary to take the record of our Lord's public ministry and read it into the record of His birth in order to discover the cross. The cross is already there! When we read the record aright, we perceive that the cross occupies a central place in the Nativity story as well as in the accounts of His later life and ministry. I once saw a picture which showed Jesus as a little boy running out of the house to meet Joseph coming from the carpenter shop. With characteristic childish joy and vivacity He ran toward the good man with His little arms outstretched. The bright sun shining down upon Him threw the shadow of a cross upon His pathway. The picture was drawn from the artist's imagination, but it suggests a spiritual truth. It coincides with the Christmas Gospel in making plain to us that from His earliest childhood the cross lay athwart the pathway of Jesus.

I. The Cross Is Seen in the Designations Applied to Mary's Child.

The names applied to our Lord in the Christmas story and the various references to His mission in the world clearly reveal the cross. The angel of the Lord said to Joseph: "And she shall bring forth a son; and thou shalt call his name JESUS; for it is he that shall save his people from their sins." The name and the explanation are one. The name JESUS means "Jehovah is salvation." The interpretation given is that "he shall save his people from their sins." Of course the messenger of God knew *how* Jesus should save His people from their sins. In bestowing the name JESUS upon Mary's Son, the Most High God indicated the redemptive mission of the Son which was to be accomplished in His atoning death for sinners upon the cross. The angel-herald gave the same message to the shepherds: "Behold, I bring you good tidings of great joy which shall be to all the people: for there is born to you this day in the city of David a Saviour, who is Christ the Lord." Christ, the Anointed One, the Messiah, was born a Saviour to all the people. Again the title of Saviour implies the manner in which He would perform His saving work; it implies the cross. Zacharias held this conception of the Messiah's mission and so defined it in his prediction concerning the prophetic office of his son who was to be the Forerunner of the Messiah:

"Yea and thou, child, shalt be called the prophet of the Most High:
For thou shalt go before the face of the Lord to make ready his ways;
To give knowledge of salvation unto his people
In the remission of their sins."

The remission of the sins of the people of God implies the sacrifice for sins made by the Son of God when He offered up Himself on Calvary's cross.

The cross stands for the fact of humiliation as well as for the remission of sins. Hence this other word which Matthew connects with the fulfilment of prophecy likewise carries its implication of the cross:

"Behold, the virgin shall be with child, and shall bring forth a son,
And they shall call his name Immanuel; which is, being interpreted,
God with us."

The birth of Jesus Christ marked the incarnation of the Son of God. The little babe lying in the Bethlehem manger is "God with us." As the meaning of the lowly manger scene becomes clear to us, we have an understanding of the humiliation of God. How many of earth's royal children are born amidst such lowly and shameful surroundings? And yet God's Son, the Lord of Glory, was born into the world of a humble peasant woman, in a rude cattle shed, amidst circumstances of poverty, suffering and neglect. Surely the manger was fashioned from the same kind of wood as the cross!

Matthew in telling the story of the return of the holy family from Egypt says that they "withdrew into the parts of Galilee, and came and dwelt in a city called Nazareth; that it might be fulfilled which was spoken through the prophets that he should be called a Nazarene." We know of no specific prophecy in the Old Testament which designates the Messiah as the "Nazarene", but the general ideas associated with the term are readily found. Isaiah's great prophecy concerning the Suffering Servant contains the root ideas of the term. "He was despised, and rejected of men; a man of sorrows, and acquainted with grief: and as one from whom men hide their face he was despised; and we esteemed him not." The designation "Nazarene" carried with it the stigma of reproach; it suggested the idea of rejection, even as Jesus was later rejected by His own people of Nazareth. Thus another outstanding fact connected with the cross is suggested here. Christ was crucified by a nation which rejected Him as the divinely appointed Messiah. He was regarded as a Nazarene, treated with contempt, and compelled to bear the reproach of the cross.

II. The Cross Is Seen in the Events Connected With His Birth.

The manger cradle represents the same kind of humiliation as the cross. The Christian Church has learned to sing, "In the cross of Christ I glory," and the Church has learned to glory in the lowly manger birth of her Lord, but the glory of the manger is one with the glory of the cross. Luke tells us that Mary "brought forth her first-born son; and she wrapped him in swaddling clothes, and laid him in a manger, because there was no room for them in the inn."

Humanly speaking, the manger birth was a necessity because the mother was crowded out of a more comfortable place. Of course the purposes of God were being fulfilled, but even so the human agencies of rejection were at work. It is not our thought that Joseph and Mary were maliciously kept out of the inn; they were not forcibly ejected; they were not turned away because they were not wanted. It was the result of the combination of unusual yet perfectly natural circumstances. The little town was full of people who had come to register for taxation purposes. The inn was quickly filled, and Joseph and Mary were not the only ones who were turned away. The sad fact is the people did not know of His coming; they were not ready to receive Him; the world was so completely absorbed in its own affairs that there was no general preparation for the greatest event of all time.

In the same way, Christ is crowded out to-day. One pastor of a large city church wrote this message for his Christmas bulletin entitled "The Christmas Paradox". "Too many Christians allow their absorption in the 'by-products' of Christmas: business, social fellowship, and gayety—to crowd from their lives the worship of the Holy Child, without Whom we would have no Christmas. One manifestation of this absorption is depleted congregations during the very season when the churches ought to be most crowded. This is the paradox of Christmas. Let us not become so wearied by the endless round of material interests that we have neither strength nor inclination to worship, during the Christmas season, at the altar of the Church of Jesus Christ." Multitudes of people who are more thoughtful, kind and charitable to their friends and neighbors during the Christmas season than at any other time of the year are yet so busy and preoccupied with their own plans and activities that Christ is crowded out. The besetting sin of our generation is that of indifference, neglect and unbelief intensified and broadened by the passion of preoccupation and absorption with worldly things. The inn in a better day, not packed with people brought there because a heathen emperor wanted more money, would have had room for Mary and Joseph and the Saviour of the world.

The prediction of Simeon in the temple at Jerusalem certainly throws the cross into clear focus. His prophetic words are: "Behold, this child is set for the falling and rising of many in Israel; and for a sign which is spoken against; yea and a sword shall pierce through thine own soul; that thoughts out of many hearts may be revealed." The offense of the cross is here; likewise the sufferings of the cross, the rejection of the cross, and the judgment of the cross. Christ was spoken against. He was called a gluttonous man and a wine-bibber, a blasphemer, an ally of Beelzebub the prince of devils by the religious leaders of the nation. He was mocked and bullied and reviled, even when He hung upon the cross, by the leaders and by the people. Simeon's words anticipated what came to pass, and later events themselves served to unfold the meaning of his prophetic utterance.

The gifts offered to the Christ Child in the house at Bethlehem are suggestive of His sufferings to come. This is especially true of the gift of myrrh. The Church has long held this gift to be emblematic of the true Humanity of Jesus, referring particularly to His death and burial. So we are told that another good man, one Nicodemus by name, came bringing "a mixture of myrrh and aloes" with which to inter the dead body of Jesus.

The cross of Christ also stands for the wicked envy, cruel hatred, and murderous sin which goads some men in their opposition to the Son of God. King Herod's attempt to destroy Mary's Son vividly reveals this dark picture of the cross. The evil-hearted man trembled on his throne at Jerusalem when he first heard tidings of the birth of the "King of the Jews". He feared a rival claimant for his blood-stained throne. His crafty mind immediately formed a plan whereby this rival would be destroyed. When this plan was thwarted by the higher obedience of the Wise-men, he put into execution the bloody attempt to catch Mary's child in the general slaughter of Bethlehem babies. This black-hearted vileness, this awful corruption of sin which poisoned the soul of Herod later hounded to the death the Doer of Good and nailed Him to the cross. Christ is being crucified afresh in many lands to-day where rulers and people still wield the bloody weapons of cruel hatred against innocent, helpless victims of atrocious warfare. The light and love of Christmas still shows the depths of man's degradation and sin; and awful crimes committed by those who do not know Christ as Saviour and Lord.

III. The Cross Is Seen in the Sufferings of the Parents and Others.

The cross of Christ also stands for suffering: innocent suffering, spiritual suffering, vicarious suffering. We find that the Infancy Gospel is not lacking in these elements of crucial suffering. For the cross is seen in the sufferings of Mary, Joseph, and others. Mary's sufferings began with the annunciation. The record is that "she was greatly troubled at the saying, and cast in her mind what manner of salutation this might be." She suffered the anguish of a deeply troubled spirit—the acutest form of suffering known to pure, sensitive souls. The mystery of the miraculous conception, the promised greatness of the Child, the strange position in which she was placed in her relationship to Joseph would naturally cause a high-souled woman like Mary to suffer acute anguish of spirit. The singular blessing conferred upon her inevitably carried with it an unusual accompaniment of suffering. The greatest blessings always entail the greatest suffering.

Joseph likewise suffered an exquisite torture of soul. We need only allow our minds to dwell upon the human elements in the story to perceive the delicate and difficult situation in which Joseph was placed. Naturally he would be sorely distressed and dismayed when he learned of Mary's strange secret. He could not believe his ears; he did not understand; he was greatly troubled. His first thought was to do all that could be done to save the family name from disgrace and shame. But even while his tortured mind thought upon these things, an angel of the Lord appeared to him and made plain the painful mystery. "Fear not," the angel said, "to take unto thee Mary thy wife: for that which is conceived in her is of the Holy Spirit." His suffering spirit was soothed by the revealing dream and he arose from his sleep, and did as the angel of the Lord commanded him. But this did not mark the end of his sufferings. The arduous journey from Nazareth to Bethlehem which brought such discomfort and distress to his young wife naturally lay heavily upon his sympathetic spirit. How would the noble man feel when he could find no refuge for his suffering wife in the inn, and was compelled to take her for the birth of her first-born child into a common stable! Soon after followed the troublesome days and fearful nights when they must be cautious and vigilant in order to save the child's life from the wicked Herod. The hazardous and trying journey to Egypt brought its share of anguish; likewise the sojourn in a strange land, and the return journey to Nazareth. Not unlike some modern parents whose minds are haunted with fears and forebodings of the evil threatenings and villainous depredations of kidnapers, the parents of the infant Saviour were robbed of the sweet joy of peaceful, happy home-centered experiences with their first little baby. Surely the parents of Jesus had their daily cross to bear in cherishing and protecting the little life of Him Who was to be the Life of the world.

But this is not all. Others, known and unknown, suffered with the devout parents. Simeon, of course, did not escape. His own anguished spirit was poured out in the words he uttered concerning the trials of Messiah and the sufferings of Mary. Simeon was not an actor; he was a prophet. His words were a burden upon his own heart before he expressed them to others. The coming of Messiah filled the old prophet's soul with the peace of consolation, but his "Nunc Dimittis" has the same undertone detected in all the other Christmas songs, namely, the clear, sweet note of suffering. Even so the Wise-men must have suffered in silence when they perceived the craftiness and malicious intent of Herod. They would go back to their own country hoping and praying that no harm would befall the beautiful child and the noble parents whom they found in the friendly house of Bethlehem. Let the tender-hearted Jeremiah describe the bitter anguish of those unknown mothers of Bethlehem whose little ones were sacrificed on the cross of innocent suffering.

> "A voice was heard in Ramah,
> Weeping and great mourning,
> Rachel weeping for her children;
> And she would not be comforted, because they are not."

And let this traditional folksong of the Mountain Whites entitled, "And the Trees Do Moan," enable us to perceive more clearly the glorious shame of the place of the Cross in Christmas.

> "In the valley of Judea,
>   Cold and wintry blown,
> Christ was born one frosty morning,
>   And the trees do moan.

Darkened skies, and men a-stumbling—
  High above there shone
One bright star a-moving Eastward,
  Where the trees do moan.

Herod and the ruling Romans
  Stately sat upon the throne,
Sent the soldiers out a-looking,
  And the trees do moan.

Mary took her little Baby,
  Set out all alone;
Down in Egypt-land they tarried,
  Where the trees do moan.

Jesus then became a carpenter,
  Worked with wood and stone,
Nails He drove and cross-arms fashioned,
  And the trees do moan.

There one day while in the forest black,
  One tree He picked for His own,
A Christmas tree an ever-green one,
  And the trees do moan."